Dr. Gary Collins

FAMILY TALK

VISION HOUSE
PUBLISHERS
Santa Ana, California 92705

Family Talk

Copyright © 1978 by Vision House Publishers, Santa Ana, California 92705.

Library of Congress Catalog Card Number 78-50854
ISBN 0-88449-029-7

Contents

Foreword

Several years ago the editors of a national magazine sent one of their top reporters on a trip to discover what was happening to the modern family. For weeks the reporter traveled, conducting interviews with family life experts, college professors and students, wife-swappers, clergymen, residents in communes, gatherers of statistics, and people who were wandering through shopping centers or out in the streets. "The family today is very much alive," the reporter wrote following this fact-finding trip, "but it is under heavy attack. There is a shooting war against the family; a war waged in the press, on TV, on the lecture platform. It is waged by angry women's libbers, by practitioners on the fringes of the encounter group movement, by student leaders and by college professors." It is also waged, we might add, by grade-school teachers, book publishers, and sometimes by clergymen and parents whose lack of active concern about family disintegration ultimately contributes to a breakdown in family unity and a destruction of traditional family values.

In one major attempt to understand the forces undermining families and to strengthen the modern family unit, over two thousand evangelical church leaders gathered in St. Louis, Missouri, not long ago for a weeklong Continental Congress on the Family. The Congress was conceived and directed by J. Allan Peterson, President of Family Concern.

I served as program director and subsequently edited five books containing most of the speeches that had been presented by the numerous experts who addressed the Congress.°

One of the major outcomes of the Congress was the preparation of a document which attempted to express our united concern about the state of the family and to summarize Biblical teachings on family life and related issues. In preparing this "Affirmation on the Family," we first wrote to approximately one hundred Christian family life specialists asking for their suggestions. From this survey a rough-draft statement was prepared, which was revised by a six-person committee who labored over each phrase of the document during an all-day work session. The rewritten statement was then distributed to all participants at the Congress on the Family, and they in turn were invited to give their written reactions. Over eight hundred people chose to do so, and these recommendations and suggestions were used in preparation of the final affirmation on the family. The completed document, therefore, had the direct input of almost one thousand people.

Those of us who worked most directly on this document occasionally found ourselves involved in stimulating and sometimes heated conversations about the status of the family. At one point it was suggested that someone should write a scholarly commentary on the Affirmation. As I pondered this it seemed that a study book for family discussion would be better. There are many commentaries and "how-to-do-it" books in print today, but books *about* families written *for* families to study together are virtually nonexistent. Such is the purpose of this volume. It is meant to be a guide for families who recognize the importance of

---

°*It's OK to Be Single, Make More of Your Marriage, The Secrets of Our Sexuality, Living and Growing Together: The Christian Family Today,* and *Facing the Future: The Church and Family Together*—all edited by Gary Collins and published by Word Books in 1976.

talking together about their own family life, marriage, view of sex, and related issues.

As indicated above, roughly one thousand people made some contribution to the production of this book, but there are several persons who had a special involvement. First are those who worked with me in writing the Affirmation on the Family: Gladys Hunt (InterVarsity Christian Fellowship), Denny Rydberg (Youth Specialties), Lars Granberg (Hope College), Cleveland MacDonald (Cedarville College), and Coleman Kerry (Friendship Baptist Church, Charlotte, N.C.). My close friend and associate, Lawrence Tornquist, coordinated much of the committee's activities and worked diligently on the project during the days when the Congress on the Family was in session. After the book was completed, a group of families (those of Marvin and Sandra Brickert, Darwin and Annette Adams, Wallace and Dilys Warning, Kenneth and Phyllis Nordloff, and Charles and Sophia DeLonghi) all from the Village Church in Barrington, Illinois, carefully tested the materials in their own homes and made suggestions which were extremely helpful. In addition, my secretary, Georgette Sattler, typed and retyped the manuscript in her usual efficient manner. To all these people I am extremely grateful.

Most significant to me, however, has been my own family, who first reacted to the material in this book and made some helpful recommendations for improvement. My wife Julie is a devoted helpmeet, a competent colaborer, a superb wife and mother, and my most insightful but gentle critic. Our two preteen daughters have (like their mother) stuck with me through the writing of many books, and they perpetually challenge my skills, competence, and self-concept as a father. One of my greatest desires is that they will grow into godly women who have Christ-centered families of their own. It is to them that this book is affectionately dedicated.

—Gary R. Collins

How to Use This Book

This book has been written for individuals to read, for families (including singles and couples without children in the home) to read and discuss together, and for use by church or other study groups interested in family-related issues.

For those individuals or families who read the book apart from group discussion, I suggest that the portion of the Affirmation at the beginning of each section be read first. If you are in a family, ask, "What does this mean?" Sometimes this leads to lively and helpful discussion, especially if this portion of the Affirmation is misunderstood or not accepted by some family member.

Next, read the Bible portion. I recommend that *The Living Bible* or some other easy-reading Bible be used for this reading. Following this, read the book commentary—out loud if you are in a family. Take turns letting different family members read both the Bible passage and the portion from this book. If children are present, discuss the "family questions" as a group. If no children are present, discuss the "questions for adults" as a group. Allow each person to express an opinion and to respond to the opinions of others. If you are alone, take the time to ponder each question by yourself. When you are finished, spend a few minutes in prayer, perhaps following the "prayer suggestions" which are given with each daily reading. In all of this try to encourage open, light-hearted discussion which brings in humor when appropriate but doesn't overlook the serious nature of the subject matter. The goal is to let these readings be informative, thought-provoking, and fun, rather than letting them become ponderous and boring.

In the back of the book is a study guide. For maximum interest and benefit, we suggest that adults meet once a week (perhaps as a church group on Sunday) to discuss the questions in the study guide. (Teenagers can have their own discussion group.) Then individual families can go through the six readings that comprise each section in the main part of the book. When the group meets again, discuss what your families learned during the previous week and consider the questions for the week which follows. Used in this way, the book can be a ten-week church-family study program. Each week there is a study-guide group discussion followed by six individual discussions in the family.

One comment is appropriate before you turn to the main part of this book. Some of the sections deal explicitly (but tastefully, we believe) with the specifics of such issues as human sexuality, abortion, birth control, and sexual deviance. Parents may want to read these various sections privately before they are discussed in the family. The Bible, of course, deals with most of these issues, and it is the author's belief that such topics should be discussed openly and without embarrassment in the home and in the church. In that way our children can learn Biblical values and accurate facts which they might not get otherwise. This is the basis of solid families which honor God and bring happiness into homes like yours.

Affirmation on the Family*

PART 1

Introduction

We, members of the Church of Jesus Christ and participants in the 1975 Continental Congress on the Family, affirm our belief in the one eternal, triune God who is Creator, Sustainer, Savior, and Lord of the universe. We express our gratitude for His great salvation and rejoice in the fellowship He has given with Himself and with other believers. We are deeply concerned about the deteriorating state of the family. We confess we have failed to give sufficient attention to our own families. We dedicate ourselves anew to the task of strengthening families in our homes, churches, communities, and nations. We affirm the divine inspiration and authority of the Bible in its entirety as the foundation on which we seek to build stronger marriages and better family relationships.

---

*Copyright © Family '76 (Omaha, Nebraska). Reprinted with permission.

The Origin and Purpose of Marriage

We believe that marriage was instituted by God at the beginning of the human race and was designed to involve the total, lifelong commitment of a man and woman to God and to each other. Therefore, marriage is an honorable status involving the privileges and responsibilities of mutual submission, companionship, respect, fidelity, sexual fulfillment, and procreation. It is a joyful joining of lives at many levels and provides the opportunity for mature love so vital to the wholeness of persons.
(Gen. 2:18-25; Exod. 20:14; Matt. 19:4-6; Eph. 5:21-33; 1 Cor. 7:1-5; 1 Pet. 3:1-7.)

PART 2

The Uniqueness of Christian Marriage

We affirm Christian marriage as a unique husband-wife relationship modeled after Christ's relationship to the Church. In Christian marriage, the husband and wife strive to become one spiritually, intellectually, emotionally, and physically, and to function interdependently as equals in accordance with Biblically prescribed roles. The husband is head of the wife. He is responsible to love her as Christ loved the Church and as he loves himself. The husband and wife dedicate themselves to the well-being of each other, cleaving, providing, and encouraging each other in their God-given freedom to develop their own gifts and abilities. The husband and wife are joint-heirs with Christ and share equally "in joy and in sorrow, in plenty and in want, in sickness and in health." The wife submits herself to her husband, loves him, and respects him. Christian marriage is meant to be a lifelong relationship between one man and one woman, indissoluble except by death.
(Matt. 19:1-12; 1 Cor. 7:10-15; Gal. 3:27, 28; Eph. 5:21-33; 1 Pet. 3:7; Prov. 31:10-31.)

PART 3

Divorce and Remarriage

We affirm the permanence of marriage as the intent of God. We believe that divorce is contrary to God's intention for marriage. Divorce is also a profound human tragedy, leaving a legacy of anguish, bitterness, loneliness, a sense of failure, and a deep fear of close personal relations. We regret the ease with which divorces are attained and believe that easy divorce and remarriage are among the factors contributing to the breakdown of family life. We believe that reconciliation is an alternative superior to divorce. The remarriage of divorced persons is inconsistent with the plan of God for mankind, but in the opinion of some believers, may be permitted because of divine grace and as a specific manifestation of the forgiveness and new beginnings offered mankind by the Christian gospel. The Church must be a community of compassion, love, healing, and forgiveness for divorced, separated, and remarried persons. The Church must also attempt to prevent divorce by clearly and persistently setting forth the Biblical teachings on marriage and sex relations, and by providing a therapeutic community of believers.
(Gen. 2:24; Matt. 19:1-9; 1 Cor. 7:10-14, 39; Rom. 7:2-4.)

PART 4

Children and Parents

We affirm that children, natural and adopted, are a heritage from God, given in sacred trust. They are not to be abused or neglected. Children are not pawns of the Church, state, or parents. Every child deserves to have a warm, caring relationship with a mother and father, the opportunity to develop a healthy self-esteem through loving parents, and the opportunity to be nurtured in an environment which models Christian behavior and values. We believe that the roles of parents include providing for their children's growth (mentally, physically, spiritually, and socially), and teaching them from the Word of God in a spirit of Christian love and nurture. Parents, together, are responsible to teach spiritual truth and other information by word of mouth and by example. They are to discipline in a firm, consistent, loving manner in the home. The role of the child includes becoming an obedient learner who is being trained to become a mature adult able to exercise wise and responsible discernment in making decisions. Children are to honor their parents, to obey them as they would obey the Lord, and to care for their needs in old age.

PART 5

Family Life

Each member of the Christian family has spiritual gifts which are to be discovered, developed, and used to glorify God and strengthen each other within the family. We deeply regret the breakdown in family closeness and order, and we urge mothers and especially fathers to resume their God-ordained roles as leaders in the home. We oppose the unhealthy influences which seek to exploit children through pornography, drug abuse, and unethical advertising. We are deeply concerned about the harmful effects of television, films, and printed news media, the lack of discipline and poor adult example in home and school, and the breakdown of family unity and cohesion. We urge parents and schools to raise and teach children in a climate of mature love, respect, and discipline. We urge churches to give priority attention to the task of equipping parents to provide homes in which the spiritual, psychological, intellectual, and social development of children is of crucial importance.
(Gen. 1:27, 28; Exod. 20:12; Deut. 5:16; 6:4-25; Prov. 1:8; 6:20; 10:1; 20:11; 22:6; 31:10-31; Acts 5:1-11; 18:1-4,

24-28; Rom. 16:3-5; 1 Cor. 11:11; Eph. 5:21-33; 6:1-4; Col. 3:20, 21, 24; Heb. 5:12-14; 1 Tim. 5:3, 4; 2 Tim. 1:5; 3:15; Tit. 2:4.)

PART 6

The Single Person

We agree that the single life is a valid lifestyle for many Christians and one to which some have been called by God. Singleness and celibacy are, for some persons, gifts from God, preferable to marriage, and conducive to greater personal and spiritual development. Many other single persons desire to marry but find no suitable mate for reasons beyond their control. We agree that the local church is intended to be the family of all God's people. We urge churches, individuals, and families to be sensitive to the needs of the single, divorced, and widowed persons in their fellowship and to help them develop a personal ministry and to establish meaningful relationships within the church family.
(Psa. 68:6; Matt. 19:12; 1 Cor. 7:7, 8, 25-27, 32-35.)

The Widowed and Elderly

We affirm that widows and widowers are to be respected, honored, and accepted fully as equals in the body of believers. We are greatly disturbed by the dishonor and difficulties experienced by the aged and widowed in our society. Family members are to honor and care for the widowed, especially those who are elderly. The Church also has responsibility to nurture and, where appropriate, to minister to the elderly, neglected, lonely, and needy in a spirit of Christian acceptance and concern.
(Job 12:12; Psa. 71:9; Prov. 16:31; 23:22; 1 Tim. 5:1-16; Tit. 2:3-5.)

PART 7

Human Sexuality

The human body and the capacity for sexual relationship, enjoyment, and reproduction are God's gifts to be received in an attitude of thanksgiving, wonder, and joyful worship. We rejoice that God created male and female as sexual beings and we affirm that sexual intercourse within marriage is good, desirable, honorable, and consistent with personal holiness. Parents are to convey such attitudes to children along with providing factual information. Parents and churches have a God-assigned responsibility to provide moral guidance by word and by example so that God's gift of sex will be used in ways honoring Jesus Christ. We deplore distorted, unbiblical, and sinful sexual attitudes and practices, both within and outside marriage, which contribute to the breakdown of the family. We resolve to resist the moral decline in our society, to teach that sex is to be enjoyed with mutual respect and fulfillment within marriage, and to proclaim that ultimate control results from Christian maturation, which is brought about by the power of the Holy Spirit through the fellowship of the faithful and through happy, useful service to Christ.

(Gen. 1:26-31; Deut. 5:18; 6:1-25; 1 Sam. 2:22; Psa. 139:13-18; Prov. 1:8-10; 5:18, 19; 6:20; 7:27; 1 Cor. 6:14-20; 7:1-6; Eph. 6:4; 1 Thes. 4:1-8; 1 Tim. 4:3-5; Heb. 13:4.)

PART 8

Homosexuality

We affirm that sexual unions between persons of the same sex are unbiblical and sinful, a perversion of the divine plan of the Creator. We oppose attempts by such homosexual unions to form unisex families through adoption, or foster-parenthood of children.

(Lev. 18:22; 20:13; Rom. 1:17; 1 Cor. 6:9; 1 Tim. 1:10.)

While we acknowledge that the Bible teaches homosexuality to be sinful, we recognize that a homosexual orientation can be the result of having been sinned against. We oppose the unjust and unkind treatment given to homosexuals by individuals, society, and the Church, and we urge the Church as the Body of Christ to accept such individuals as needing understanding, forgiveness, encouragement, and spiritual support.
(Rom. 2:1; Matt. 18:11; 1 Thes. 4:8, 9).

We pledge ourselves to minister to those who are homosexually oriented in order to help them to change their lifestyle in a manner which brings glory to God.
(1 Cor. 6:11; 2 Cor. 5:17; Rom. 8:1.)

Birth Control

We acknowledge that Christians differ in their views on birth control, and we respect these differences in the light of Scripture's almost total silence on this subject. God, at the time of creation, commanded mankind to be fruitful and multiply, and we rejoice in the birth of children as a heritage and gift from God. We are deeply concerned about the realities of overpopulation, world hunger, and the harmful effects that overpopulation can have on the environment and on individual families. We encourage Christian couples to limit the size of their families in a way that is not at variance with Biblical teaching, and to keep family size to the number of children that can be nourished and taught effectively.
(Gen. 1:38; 38:9, 10; Psa. 127:4, 5; Prov. 22:6; Eph. 5:17; 1 Tim. 5:8.)

PART 9
Abortion

We acknowledge that Christians differ in their view concerning the time when personhood begins, but we agree that God has admonished us to choose life instead of death, and has set penalties for those who would, even accidentally, cause a pregnant woman to be injured in such a way that an unborn child is harmed. We believe that compassion for distressed mothers and families, and concern for unborn children, require us to offer spiritual guidance and material solace consistent with the teachings of God's Word. We urge the Church to influence the social-moral climate in which unintended pregnancies occur. We see no grounds on which Christians who are concerned for all human life and for the well-being of the family can condone the free and easy practice of abortion as it now exists in our society. At the same time, we exhort the Church to show compassion for those who suffer because of the abortion experience.

(Exod. 21:22; Psa. 8; Psa. 139:13-18; Jer. 1:4, 5; Luke 1:39-66; 10:30-37.)

PART 10
The Christian Family and the Church

We affirm that the family as a unit is not self-sufficient and self-contained as a body of believers. Rather, the family has need of continuing support from other families and from individuals within the Body. The local Church is a company of believers who exist for fellowship, worship, teaching, and the development of spiritual gifts to the end that God will be glorified and the Body of Christ edified. As part of the universal Body of Christ, the local Church is an extended family composed of nuclear families. The Church exists to support, nurture, and equip individuals and families for growth in discipleship (including evangelism) and effective functioning. We urge, therefore, that families become involved actively in the local Church and that they pray, worship, and serve Christ together. We urge churches to minister to families and individuals in creative ways which build Church and family unity, prepare young people for mate selection and marriage, educate families in effective family living, assist family members and individuals in their spiritual and personal growth, and give support in times of stress or special need.

(Matt. 16:18; Acts 2:41-47; 4:32-35; Rom. 8:16, 17; 1 Cor. 6:15; Eph. 3:15; 5:30; Col. 1:18.)

To Marilynn and Janice . . .

Many daughters have done nobly,
But you excel them all. . . .
A woman who fears the Lord,
She shall be praised.

— Proverbs 31:29, 30 NASB

Part 1

The Bible & the Family

It's well-known that the modern family is in trouble. Those old pictures of families together in the parlor enjoying each other, or working together on chores in the kitchen, just can't be updated and made to fit this last quarter of the twentieth century. Marriages are breaking up at steadily increasing rates, and in numerous homes the family members just can't seem to get along with each other. These days about the only thing which pulls people into the same room at home is an impersonal TV set, which often teaches values in living color which parents don't want their children to learn at all! Frequently families don't even sit down to eat together—we grab a burger on the run as family members scurry about their individual activities.

Literally hundreds of books and probably thousands of articles have been written to analyze and help reverse this decline in family unity and stability. Marriage and family enrichment courses, counseling, encounter groups, seminars, study programs—all of these have probably had some positive effect on strengthening the family. Nevertheless, as Christians we must recognize that the basis for modern family stability must be the ancient religion of Christianity. God created us in the first place, and He is still in charge of the world. Marriage, families, sex, and child-rearing were all God's idea, and in the pages of the Bible He has given us some broad outlines for marital stability and family unity.

During this first week we will discuss the Bible and its importance in helping marriages and families to grow, mature, and get along better.

Day 1

We, members of the Church of Jesus Christ . . . affirm our belief in the one eternal triune God who is Creator, Sustainer, Savior, and Lord of the universe. We express our gratitude for His great salvation and rejoice in the fellowship He has given with Himself and with other believers.

Read: John 1:1-3, 10-14

This is a book about families. It is a book about family problems, about how families can get along better, enjoy each other, and do things together.

Have you ever wondered how families got started in the first place? According to the Bible, the family was God's idea. He made the world out of nothing, and then put the first man and woman together in a little family. In the beginning this was a happy family, which was what God wanted, but then the family members decided to disobey God. That got them into all kinds of trouble, and ever since then family members have found that it isn't always easy to get along with each other. Sometimes we disagree, argue, say unpleasant things, and even fight with the people in our families. One of the reasons for this is that people today still disobey God. They don't pay proper attention to Him and aren't very interested in pleasing Him.

But God is interested in us. He made us and He keeps us alive. He even has His own family, and He would like all of us to be His children.

Many years ago a man named Nicodemus came late one night to talk with Jesus. "What you need," Jesus told Nicodemus, "is to be born into God's family."

"How can I do that?" Nicodemus asked. "I'm a grown man. I can't become a baby and be born all over again."

Nicodemus was all confused, but Jesus explained what He meant.

When we are born on earth, we have very small bodies. These bodies, of course, grow larger, and someday they will die. We are only in our earthly bodies and earthly families for a few years. When we are born into God's family, however, we are given the promise that even after we die on earth we will go on living with God forever.

As long as we are here in this world, we can get into God's family whenever we want. Tell God you've disobeyed Him and are sorry. Ask Him to forgive your sins through Christ and to take you into His family. If you believe that God can do this, He will. Then you will be a member of two families—God's family and your earthly family.

Your earthly family includes your brothers, your sisters, your parents, and (if you are old enough) your children. God's family is a heavenly one, in which God is the Father and the family members consist of all those people who are God's children.

When Jesus came to earth many years ago, He died on the cross as a punishment for our sins and thereby made it possible for us to be members of God's family. Many people today are members of only one family, yet you can be a member of two families if you want to.

Questions

a *For Family Discussion:* Do you have trouble getting along in your family? Why? How could you get along better? What could each of you do tomorrow to help you get along better? Are you all members of God's family? If not, how could you get into the family of God?

b *For Adult Discussion:* Do you agree that God is interested in your family? Why? Are you a member of God's family? If not, why not? If so, how does this influence your earthly family life? How should it influence your family life?

Prayer Suggestions

Thank God for making families. Thank Him for your family. Ask Him to help each family member to be willing to work at getting along better. If you have never asked to become a part of God's family, tell Him of your desire. Ask Him to make clear to you what this means.

Day 2

We are deeply concerned about the deteriorating state of the family. We confess we have failed to give sufficient attention to our own families. We dedicate ourselves anew to the task of strengthening families in our homes, churches, communities, and nations.

Read: 2 Chronicles 7:11-16

This Bible reading tells us about an event which took place hundreds of years ago. King Solomon and his workers had built a house for God. It was a beautiful building, made with the best stone and wood, filled with fine carvings, and decorated with gold, silver, iron, and brass. Building the house (or Temple, as it was called) had taken a lot of work. Of course in those days there were no bulldozers, electric saws, trucks, or tractors. Everything had to be done by hand, and for this reason it had taken many years to get the building finished.

Finally the work was done, and now great crowds of people came together to celebrate and to praise God. As all the people watched, King Solomon prayed, and this is part of what he said:

> O Lord God of Israel, there is no god like you in heaven or earth, for you are loving and kind, and you keep your promises to your people if they do their best to do your will. . . . But is it possible that God would really live on earth? Why, even the skies and the highest heavens cannot contain you, much less this Temple I have built! And yet, O Lord my God, you have heard and answered my request: Please watch over this Temple night and day—this place you have promised to live in— and as I . . . pray, whether by night or by day, please listen to me and answer my request (1 Kings 8:23, 27-29).

After the celebration was over and the people had gone home, God spoke to the king one night and made a promise: "If my people will humble themselves and pray, and search for me, and turn from their wicked ways, I will hear them from heaven and forgive their sins and heal their land."

God thought that the king's land needed healing. Do you think *our* country is sick and needs healing today? Even in a rich land like ours many people are poor. Crime is getting worse and worse, people's minds are filled with thoughts which do not please God, and many people ignore God altogether. But one of the biggest problems today is with families—many of them can't get along. Mothers and fathers argue, kids fight, teenagers don't respect their parents, grandparents are ignored or treated badly, parents are cruel to their children, and in many homes, family members don't even like being with each other. These families are sick and need healing.

If your family doesn't have a lot of problems, that's good. But almost all families have some problems, and we should be finding ways to make families better—our own families and the families in our churches, neighborhoods, and country.

What can we do to make our families better? For one thing, we can think about our problems and work at solving them. But we can also remind ourselves of God's promise to King Solomon. If we humble ourselves, pray, look to God, and stop sinning, He will hear our prayers, forgive us, and heal our land—and its families.

God doesn't really need a house to live in. He's too big for that. But He is interested in your house and mine. He wants to be with us in our homes and to heal the problems in our families. Can we make our homes and families a place where He would feel welcome?

Questions

a *For Family Discussion:* What does it mean to humble ourselves? Do you know what it means to pray, to search for God, and to turn from evil ways? How can you do each of these things in your family? How can you make your house more like a place where God would feel welcome?

b *For Adult Discussion:* What are the issues, pressures, or problems in your home that need healing? As adults, what can you do to strengthen your family and the families in your church, community, and nation? Try to be specific and practical.

Prayer Suggestions

Thank God that He is 1) so great that He cannot be confined in a house and 2) so interested in us that He is concerned about the condition of our families and nations. Ask God to bring healing to families, including yours. Pray that He will move in our midst to strengthen families and reverse the deterioration of the family.

Day 3

We affirm the divine inspiration and authority of the Bible in its entirety as the foundation on which we seek to build stronger marriages and better family relationships.

Read: 2 Timothy 3:14-17

Have you ever wondered how the Bible got written? Do you think somebody sat down one day and decided, "I think I'll write a Bible"? No! The Bible was written by about 40 different people. They were holy men who were used by God to write in their own words what God wanted us to know (1 Peter 2:20). It took about 1600 years for the writings to be finished, and the people who wrote the different books of the Bible probably didn't even realize at the time that their writings would become so important.

As you probably know, one of these Bible writers was a man named Paul. In his early life Paul was probably a rich man who came from a fine family and had a very good education. Paul was also very religious, but he hated Christians; whenever he got the chance he made life difficult for those people who wanted to follow Christ. One day Paul and a few other men decided to go to a place called Damascus, where they hoped to capture some Christians and have them put in jail. As they traveled, a bright light suddenly shone down from heaven, and the voice of Jesus called out Paul's name. It didn't take Paul long to see that what he had been doing was wrong. Almost at once he stopped hating Christians and became one himself. Soon he was telling others about the wonderful Lord whom he had met on the road to Damascus.

After he became a Christian, Paul did a lot of preaching and traveling, and on one of his trips he met a young man named Timothy. Timothy's mother and grandmother had taught him about God in their family, and before long Timothy was traveling with Paul and preaching too.

When they were not together, Paul used to write letters to his friend Timothy, and two of these letters are in our Bible. We read from one of them today. It might have been the last letter that Paul ever wrote, since he was at the time in jail for preaching and telling people about Jesus. In this letter Paul told Timothy to keep on believing what he had been taught, and he reminded Timothy to read and study the Bible. The Bible, Paul said, was given to us by God. It

—teaches us to let Jesus Christ control our lives;

—tells us what is true;

—shows us what is wrong in our lives and helps us to do what is right;

—prepares us for the future;

—gets us ready for doing good to other people.

The Bible certainly is a very important book. Its teachings are true and useful, including what it says about marriage and the family.

Since God created us and put us into families, it is important to know what God has to say about the families which He made. In the rest of this book we will try to understand what we can learn about families by reading God's book—the Bible. We will even discover that God used Paul to give us some of the most important teachings about the family the world has ever known.

Questions

a *For Family Discussion:* Why do we study and believe the Bible? Is it possible that a book as old as the Bible could say anything important to modern people like us and families like ours? Give reasons for your answer.

b *For Adult Discussion:* Why do Christians believe in the authority of the entire Bible? (If you don't know, how could you find out?) Modern man has rejected the Bible as a source of authority. What, then, has become authoritative in place of the Bible? How do you study the Bible? How could you study it more effectively?

Prayer Suggestions

Thank God that He has given us the Bible and has not left us ignorant about His truth and His plans for us. Ask Him to teach us clearly about the family so that our families can be more like what He wants them to be.

Day 4

We believe marriage was instituted by God at the beginning of the human race and was designed to involve total, lifelong commitment of a man and woman to God and to each other.

Read: Genesis 2:7, 18-25

Have you ever seen kids play wedding? When I was very young we lived around the corner from a big Catholic church, and very often on a Saturday morning the church bells would ring to tell the neighborhood that somebody was getting married. From blocks around, the kids would come to watch the bride and groom come out of the church, and then we would scoop up the confetti and rice that had landed on the sidewalk. Sometimes we would even take the confetti (mixed with a little dirt) back home and use it to play wedding. We would throw the confetti at each other, and the only time we got into trouble was when we decided to do this in the house!

As children we had no idea how much work was involved in planning a wedding: reserving the church, sending out invitations, buying the flowers, finding someone to take the pictures, ordering the wedding cake, and everything else that has to be done. When you are planning a wedding, all of this can be very important. Since most people plan to get married only once, they like to make sure that the wedding and the reception are exactly what they want.

The first marriage in the world wasn't like this, however. There was no church, no organ, no preacher, no cake, and no bridesmaids. There weren't even any neighborhood children to scoop up the confetti. Besides the bride and groom, the only one there was God. Instead of being in vases, the flowers were still on the plants. And the bride didn't wear a long dress and veil. In fact, she didn't wear anything at all, and neither did the groom!

There was nothing wrong with this. Adam and Eve—the first groom and bride—had not sinned yet; there was nothing wrong with their bodies, and they didn't even think about being naked. God had given them to each other. He wanted them to love each other all their lives, and He wanted them to obey God together.

But Adam and Eve didn't obey God. They did what He told them not to do, and then they began to blame each other for their problems. Because of their sin, they had trouble getting along, and life became very difficult.

God doesn't want married couples to have trouble getting along today. Marriage was His idea in the first place. He wants husbands and wives to leave their parents, to form a new family, and to stay very close to each other during their whole lives. One way to do this is for married people to stay close to God and obedient to Him. Adam and Eve, the first married couple, were disobedient. It is good to remember that this is what caused all of their problems in the first place.

Questions

a *For Family Discussion:* According to the Bible reading, when a man gets married he leaves his father and mother and is joined to his wife. What does this mean? Why is this important? Why do you think God wanted Adam to have a wife? (In our next section we will discuss why people get married today.)

b *For Adult Discussion:* What kind of marriage are the children seeing in your house? Could it be better? How could your marriage (or the marriages of the people closest to you) be improved to provide a better example of what God wants marriage to be like? Be specific and practical.

Prayer Suggestions

Thank God for marriage. Think of a marriage—inside your home or without—that you know well. Pray for the husband and wife, asking God to give the couple a better marriage. Ask Him to help your children develop a healthy view of marriage.

Day 5

Marriage is an honorable status involving the privileges and responsibilities of mutual submission, companionship, respect, fidelity, sexual fulfillment, and procreation.

Read: John 2:1-12

During the thirty or more years that He lived on earth, Jesus never got married. We know that some of the disciples had wives—Peter, for example (Matthew 8:14)—but the only family Jesus ever had was his parents, brothers, and sisters.

Don't think, however, that Jesus had no interest in marriage. He spoke about it in His sermons, and the first miracle that He ever did took place at a wedding. All of the guests were having a good time at the celebration, but then somebody discovered that there was nothing left for the people to drink. This must have been very embarassing to the bride and groom, but soon Jesus heard about the problem.

"Fill up the jugs with water," He told the servants, "and then take some out for the people to drink." To the servants' surprise they found that the water had been changed into wine. And it wasn't bad-tasting wine, either. In fact, it was the best they had had all day!

In the years that followed, I wonder how often the bride and groom thought about their wedding and the miracle that Jesus did. However, Jesus was probably more interested in how the husband and wife were getting along as a married couple. In those days parents decided who young people would marry, and there weren't many divorces. It was important for couples to learn how they could live happily with each other and stay together. It is just as important today.

To help us get along better, the Bible tells us a lot about marriage. Marriage is something which pleases God. It is something desirable and very good, although we know that husbands and wives must work hard to keep having a marriage which is really happy.

Marriage can keep people from getting lonely, especially when there are no children in the home. In a really good marriage (the kind that God likes) the couple is always trying to do things for each other. They spend time together, try to make each other happy, and don't give any thought to having a new boyfriend or girlfriend. The married couple tries to think good thoughts about each other and to say nice things. They even enjoy each other's body, and ordinarily they have children whom they can love, teach, and appreciate.

Sometimes people get married for the wrong reasons. Some want to make their parents angry, others feel sorry for each other, and still others hope that marriage will make them rich, famous, or well-liked. None of these is a good reason for marrying. Marriage is very important, and we must give careful thought both to whom we will marry and to how we can get along better after we are married.

It takes a lot of effort, but marriage is worth all the work. According to the Bible, the man "who finds a wife finds a good thing; she is a blessing to him from the Lord" (Proverbs 18:22). The same can be true of the woman who finds a husband.

Questions

a *For Family Discussion:* Why do people get married? What are *good* reasons for getting married? How do we find a good marriage partner?

b *For Adult Discussion:* According to the statement which begins this chapter, marriage exists for mutual submission, companionship, respect, fidelity, sexual fulfillment, and procreation. What does each of these terms mean? Does each exist in your marriage? How can each be developed?

Prayer Suggestions

Thank God that He has taught us about marriage in the Bible. Ask Him for help in making our marriages come closer to the Biblical ideal. Ask Him to protect and guide the future mates of our children.

Day 6

It [marriage] is a joyful joining of lives at many levels and provides the opportunity for mature love so vital to the wholeness of persons.

Read: 1 Corinthians 13:1-7

When the new Burger King opened in our town several years ago, my children tried it out and came home with some happy news. "Daddy," they exclaimed, "we just *love* their hamburgers!"

Parents soon discover that children love a lot of things—ice cream, dungarees, swimming, Christmas, summer camp, kittens, parades, and days off from school. To say we "love" these things is all right, but when the Bible talks about love it means something much more and much better.

Perhaps it's the songs on the radio, the stories in books and magazines, or the plays on TV which give us wrong ideas about love. Many people seem to think that we can only love what looks pretty, feels good, and does things for us. Our family has a car like that. It looks great, feels comfortable as we ride, and usually does what we want it to do. We've even got a name for our car—but we don't love it like we love each other. On the other hand, when my wife had the flu recently she didn't look very good, I didn't want to get close enough to feel her (lest I get the flu too), and she certainly didn't do anything for me (she was lying flat on her back in bed)—but I still loved her and was very concerned because she was so sick.

If we really love someone it hardly matters what he (or she) looks like, how he makes us feel, or what he does for us. Jesus showed us this when He came to earth to die for us on the cross. He loved us even though we were sinners who didn't show much love in return.

According to the Bible, love is just about the greatest thing in the world. If you really love someone, we read, you will be kind to him, patient, never selfish, always wanting the best for him. You will stick with the person you love, even when he doesn't stick with you. You will always want to give attention, pleasure, and help to him, even when he doesn't give anything in return.

Of course this is not easy to do. Very often when somebody says an unkind word or hurts us we think of something nasty to say or do in return. I wonder if this happened to Adam and Eve. Adam was pretty excited when he first saw his new wife, but I wonder if he stopped loving her later. That has happened in a lot of marriages today. Many couples really don't understand what true love is in the first place, so before long they decide they don't love each other anymore.

If we don't love someone, what can we do about it? Well, we don't just sit around waiting for the feeling of love to come. First, we ask God to help us love with His kind of love. Then we start doing things—kind, thoughtful, and unselfish things. Soon we discover that when we are doing loving acts the *feeling* of love follows. This is good for everyone, and it pleases God. That kind of love is far better than "loving" a parade or hamburger (even if it has French fries!).

Questions

a *For Family Discussion:* Tell what love, as described in the Bible, is really like. How do we get that kind of love in our homes and marriages? If everyone in the family loved that way, how would our families be different?

b *For Adult Discussion:* How can a couple keep love alive in their marriage? Do you agree with the suggestion that true love is the result of prayer and doing loving deeds (rather than waiting for a feeling to come)? In what practical ways could you be more loving this week?

Prayer Suggestions

Jesus showed us what love is like when He was here on earth. Thank Him for His love, and for teaching us what true love is like. Ask Him to make you and your family more loving. Ask Him to help you do more loving things for others.

Part 2

How to Be Married & Like It

What does it mean to be married? That question might have been easy to answer 50 or 100 years ago, but things are different today. Confronted with a radically changing society, young couples are searching for contemporary styles of wedlock. There is *trial marriage*, for example, in which a man and woman live together and have sexual access to each other but never legalize their relationship. We used to call this "common-law marriage" or "shacking up." Sometimes this continues for life, and the couple may even raise children. *Group marriage* involves three or more people, usually heterosexual, who share together economically and sexually. *Gay marriage* has both partners of the same sex. In *open marriage* there is a swapping of sex partners.

More acceptable to Christians are *childless marriages*, in which a deliberate decision is made not to have children, *50-50 marriage*, in which husband and wife each pursue a career and share duties at home, and *communal living*, in which married couples are true to each other sexually but share everything else in a community of equals.

The increasing popularity of these and other new styles of marriage, coupled with the tendency in our society not to treat marriage seriously, can create a lot of confusion in the minds of Christian young people (and their parents). The Bible, however, clears much of this confusion by giving divine guidelines for marriage. When these Scriptures were written the culture was, if anything, more corrupt and more disrespectful of marriage than is ours today. The Word of God, therefore, is relevant even for us today. It speaks to the problems of contemporary marriage, and it can help our children to get a perspective on how to be married and like it.

Day 1

We affirm Christian marriage as a unique husband-wife relationship modeled after Christ's relationship to the Church.

Read: Ephesians 5:25-30

Several years ago our family lived for a while in Europe, and often on a Sunday afternoon, following church, we would go sightseeing. One of the places we liked to visit was a big stately cathedral which sat on a hill where it could be seen from all over the city. This church had big doors covered with carvings, and the windows were made from colored glass which gave a beautiful effect inside whenever the sun was shining outside. Some very famous people had been buried under the floor of this church, and in some of the corners there were stone statues of these people, lying down as if they were sleeping.

However, in some places the church was dusty, and outside the stones were almost black because of the dirt that had blown against the building and stuck there. Before long my children began calling this "the dirty church." I tried to tell them that they would be dirty too if they had been standing outside for 800 years without a bath—but they weren't impressed. Even now, when we talk about our time in Europe somebody in the family is sure to remind us of our visits to the dirty church.

But of course not all churches are dirty. Some are very clean and even have air conditioning. Some are very large, like the cathedrals of Europe, and some are so small that they meet in the living room of a home.

Did you know, however, that when the Bible talks about a church it almost never means a building? The church of Jesus Christ is really a group of people. The word "church" means all the people who have invited Jesus to control their lives and are a part of God's family.

The Bible tells us that Jesus Christ is in charge of the church. He cares for the church, loves it, and even died so that people who make up the church could become holy and have all their sins forgiven. The cathedrals in Europe are made of stones which are dirty, and getting dirtier, but the real church of Jesus Christ is made of people who are someday going to be holy, clean inside, and without a single fault.

Now isn't it interesting that God says our families should be like Christ's church? The Bible even talks of Jesus as a groom and the church as His bride. Just as Christ is head of the church, so the husband and father is head of the family. Just as Christ loved the church and was even willing to die for the church, so the man must love his family and be willing to give everything he has to help them improve. Just as the members should all work together in a church, so we ought to be doing this at home.

All of this begins, of course, with the husband and wife. If they are sincere followers of Jesus, their marriage should be different from marriages in which Christ is mostly ignored. Christians should study the Bible often to learn more and more about Jesus Christ and about His church. What we learn can then be brought into our own lives and marriages. It is then that we build better marriages and improve our families. That is going to make everybody happy—not just husbands and wives, but the kids as well.

Questions

a *For Family Discussion:* Tell about some of the different churches you have visited. How are they different? What are some good things about your church? In what ways do you think marriage is like Christ and His church?

b *For Adult Discussion:* How can Christ's relationship to the church be an example of a husband's relationship to his wife? How can your marriage better fit the picture of Christ and His bride, the church? Discuss one practical thing you could do this week to make your marriage more consistent with the Bible's teachings.

Prayer Suggestions

Thank God for your church and for the people who make up the church. Ask Him to help the church improve. Ask Him to help the marriages you know about (including the one in your house) become more like the closeness between Christ and His bride (the church).

Day 2

In Christian marriage, the husband and wife strive to become one spiritually, intellectually, emotionally, and physically, and to function interdependently as equals in accordance with Biblically prescribed roles.

Read: Acts 18:1-4, 24-28

How would you like to have the name Aquila? There was a man with that name living in Corinth when the Apostle Paul arrived there during one of his missionary trips. Aquila was a tentmaker, and since Paul was a tentmaker too, he went to live for a while with Aquila and his wife Priscilla.

Aquila and Priscilla must have been an interesting couple. They did a lot of things together—working in their tentmaking business, traveling, helping others (including Paul), and worshiping. Once they even risked their lives for Paul because they wanted to help so much with his missionary work (Romans 16:4). We know that Aquila and Priscilla had a church in their house (1 Corinthians 16:19), and at one time they met a preacher named Apollos whom they helped greatly. This man first heard about Jesus from Aquila and Priscilla, and after they had taught him, Apollos went to Greece, where he was used by God to preach in the churches and synagogues.

Aquila and Priscilla did almost everything together. Their two lives had become a team. This is God's plan for marriage—that two lives, those of a man and woman, will come together as a husband and wife to form a team and do things together until one of them dies.

Can you imagine what it would be like trying to ride a teeter-totter or to play tennis all by yourself? These activities need two people working together if there is to be any fun. Some husbands and wives don't realize that marriage is teamwork. They live together but they don't talk much to each other, they don't do many things together and their marriage isn't very happy. They are like two people on different teeter-totters, wondering why they aren't getting along very well or having fun together.

There are people today with some unusual ideas about marriage. Some people just live together, not bothering about a wedding, until they can decide whether to get married at all. Others live in a big house where everyone sleeps together and men keep trading wives back and forth. Sometimes people of the same sex "marry" each other— like two men or two women. None of this is pleasing to God. He wants one man and one woman to live and work together as a team that lasts for all of life.

As we will see next time, God has some special instructions for husbands and other instructions for wives. But it is important, first, to understand that marriage involves two people of the opposite sex who love each other and work to get along with each other.

This, it seems, was the kind of marriage that Aquila and Priscilla had. They enjoyed each other, appreciated each other, did things for each other, and worked together. They were always interested in pleasing God, and they tried to live their lives by obeying Him. That's what Christian marriage is really all about.

Questions

a *For Family Discussion:* Describe marriage as God intends it to be. What does it mean for a husband and wife to be a team? Why do you think Aquila and Priscilla got along so well with each other?

b *For Adult Discussion:* What is the meaning of each of the following terms in the Affirmation statement: "strive," "become one spiritually, intellectually, emotionally, physically," "function interdependently as equals"? How can each of these be put into practice? How can you get these into your marriage?

Prayer Suggestions

Thank God for people like Aquila and Priscilla who serve God together. Thank Him for other couples like that whom you may know. Ask Him to help you and your friends to have marriages in which there is real sharing together between the husband and wife. Children might ask God to help their parents' marriage to improve (even if it is good already).

Day 3

The husband is head of the wife. He is responsible to love her as Christ loved the Church and as he loves himself.

Read: Ephesians 5:21-25, 28-33

Do you remember the life story of John the Baptist? He was the son of a very old couple who were related to Jesus' mother Mary. John the Baptist traveled all around the country telling people to turn away from their sins and back to God. He urged people to be honest, baptized them, and, most important of all, told them that their Savior would be coming along very soon.

John must have been a brave man, because he boldly pointed out the sins of other people and wasn't even afraid to criticize the king. King Herod had decided one time that he liked his brother's wife better than his own, so the king divorced his wife and stole the wife of his brother. The new queen, whose name was Herodius, wasn't very happy when John the Baptist announced that what the king had done was wrong. Herodius convinced the king to have John put in jail, and then the wicked queen Herodius did something even worse.

When the king had a big birthday party, he asked Herodius' daughter to dance before all the guests. The dance pleased the king so much that he promised to give the girl whatever she wanted as a reward. "Tell him you want the head of John the Baptist on a tray," Herodius told her daughter, and that is exactly what the girl requested. The king wasn't very happy about this, but he had made a promise in front of all his guests, so he ordered the soldiers to bring in the head of John.

When John's head was cut off he died immediately—which really isn't surprising. A head without a body can't survive. There is no heart to pump blood, no lungs to breathe oxygen, no hands to bring food, and no stomach for the food after it is swallowed. The body is also useless without a head. Without a brain the body couldn't think, and neither could it see, hear, smell, taste, or breathe. To live we need both a head and a body.

When the Bible talks about Christian marriage it says that the husband is the head and the wife is the body. Both are needed for a marriage to be really successful. But some couples don't like this idea. They want the husband and wife to both be heads. They want their marriage to be like a monster with two heads and no body.

As the one head of the home, the husband has several important jobs. He must care for his wife and family, protect them, lead them, give himself to them, and meet their needs. But most important, he must love them, especially his wife. That is the husband's number one job. He is to love his wife as much as Christ loved people in the church; he should love his wife as much as he loves himself.

The husband who loves his wife that much won't deliberately hurt her, even as he wouldn't hurt himself. As head of the home the husband should try to understand his wife, help her, and apply this golden rule: husbands, treat your wife like you want to be treated yourself.

If King Herod had known this, he might have been more concerned about his first wife and less interested in stealing someone else's wife. The king would have been happier, there would have been fewer problems in the palace, and John the Baptist would have kept his head.

Questions

a *For Family Discussion:* Why did John the Baptist say that King Herod had sinned? What does it mean to say that the husband is head of the home? Why can't the husband and wife both be head of the home?

b *For Adult Discussion:* The headship of husbands is not a popular idea in our times. Can a husband be head of the home and still allow his wife freedom to develop her talents, interests, and career? Give reasons for your answer. How do you reconcile Ephesians 5:21 with Ephesians 5:22?

Prayer Suggestions

Thank God for husbands. If there is a husband in your house ask God to help him to be the Christlike head of the home. Ask God to help the husband really love his wife like Christ loves us.

Day 4

The husband and wife dedicate themselves to the well-being of each other, cleaving, providing, and encouraging each other in their God-given freedom to develop their own gifts and abilities. The husband and wife are joint-heirs with Christ and share equally "in joy and in sorrow, in plenty and in want, in sickness and in health."

Read: Ephesians 4:7, 11-13

What do you think of birthdays? Very old people seem to enjoy them, especially when they get their pictures in the paper and are asked why it is that they have lived so long. Middle-aged people try to forget them, because birthdays are a reminder that they are getting older. Children usually love them, especially if there is a party.

When I was growing up we lived in a neighborhood where just about everybody had a party to celebrate birthdays. We kids would get all dressed up and go to the place of the party, where we played games, popped balloons, made a lot of noise, won prizes, ate cake, spilled pop and ice cream, and drove the poor mothers crazy. Fathers, I noticed, weren't around very often, and now I've begun to see why—a children's birthday party can be a pretty hectic affair!

The thing I liked best about parties was the presents that I got on my birthday. I always wanted to invite a lot of guests to my parties, not because they were my friends (some of them even tried to beat me up at school), but because they would bring gifts.

We never think much about this, but birthday gifts help us to celebrate the day we came into our families on earth. Did you know that God gives us gifts too? He has adopted us into His family and given us gifts that we can use, not to amuse ourselves, but to help each other. Some Christians have a special gift of speaking, so that they are very fine preachers. Some have gifts as writers and teachers. Some are gifted counselors who can help people with their problems. Others have gifts in music or in some other area.

Every Christian has received gifts from God. The rich, the poor, the famous, the unknown—all are gifted in some way. This is also true of husbands and wives, who very often have gifts that differ from each other. The wife, for example, may be an especially good teacher, while the husband's gift comes in organizing a business or church group.

The Bible warns us not to be jealous because somebody else has a gift that we don't have. God gives each of us the gifts that are best for us and for the other Christians in the church. Our job, then, is to use our gifts and help others to do the same.

In our house, everybody agrees that I have a gift in the area of writing. But it isn't easy to write, especially when the telephone is ringing and there is a lot of noise. To help me write, therefore, my family tries not to disturb me. Later they read what I write and suggest how to make it better. They are helping me with my gift—like I try to help them with theirs.

In Christian marriage, the husband and wife help each other like this. They don't envy each other's gifts, but they work together to aid and encourage each other so that both can grow into the kinds of Christian people that God wants them to be. Married couples help each other when they are healthy or when one of them is sick, when they are rich or when they are poor, when they are happy or when they are sad. That's what makes Christian marriage so good. It takes a lot of work and it means helping each other all the time, but it can be great, even better than a birthday party!

Questions

a *For Family Discussion:* What kinds of gifts do we get from God? Why does He give them? What gifts has God given each member of your family? How can a husband and wife help each other to use their gifts?

b *For Adult Discussion:* Read Galatians 3:28. How can we all be equal in God's sight if we have different gifts and responsibilities? What are your spiritual gifts and the gifts of those in your home? In your family are you dedicated to the task of helping each other to freely develop and use your gifts?

Prayer Suggestions

Let's thank God for birthday parties and the friends we have. Let's thank Him for adopting us into His family and giving us gifts. Let's ask Him to give us the desire to help each other grow into the kinds of Christians He wants us to be.

Day 5

The wife submits herself to her husband, loves him, and respects him.

Read: 1 Peter 3:1-7

Back in the Old Testament in the book of Proverbs (31:10, 11) we read some advice for men: "If you can find a truly good wife, she is worth more than precious gems! Her husband can trust her, and she will richly satisfy his needs."

Sarah must have been a woman like this. She was very beautiful even in her old age, and she spent her life married to a rich man named Abraham. When her husband traveled, Sarah went too. When Abraham asked her to do something, she obeyed and honored her husband, who was head of the family.

While Sarah was alive, however, women weren't treated very well. In ancient times it was assumed that women weren't as good as men. If you were female, you didn't have much freedom to come or go as you liked and you couldn't get a very good education because it was thought that women were not as smart as men. Even many years after Sarah had died, the men used to say a prayer in the synagogues to thank God for making them men and not women.

Perhaps more than anything else in history, Christianity did something to change these opinions. Women aren't second best, the Bible said, but are just as good as men (Galatians 3:28). God made women, He loves them, He cares for them, and He is not pleased when they are mistreated. Husbands should know this because, as we read today, God sometimes does not answer the prayers of men who do not care for their wives or treat them kindly.

But the Bible also gives some directions for wives. They are to love God so constantly that they become beautiful people on the inside—kind and loving—even if they are not beautiful on the outside. Wives are to recognize that God put the husband in charge of the home. He is expected to love his wife and treat her well, but she is expected to let him make the final decisions because he is responsible to God for the family. Letting the husband be head of the home does not mean that women are not as good as men; it means that the wife willingly lets her partner protect and care for her so that she is free to do other things that God might want her to do.

In our house, a lot of things get discussed as a family, and other things are talked over by the parents alone. This book is one example. Before you saw it, my family read it. We talked and prayed about it together, but in the end I made the final decisions about what would be in these pages. That's because I was in charge of writing the book.

The same should be true of families. The husband and wife, with their children, work as a team, but everyone, including the wife, must happily agree that God has put the husband in charge. This is God's way. A lot of families don't like it, but the families that please God most are in homes where the husband is head, where the wife submits to him, and where both the man and woman love God, love each other, do things as a team, and bring honor to Christ by happily doing what their mate wants (Ephesians 5:21).

Questions

a *For Family Discussion:* In ancient days women weren't treated as well as men. Is this true today? Why should the wife obey her husband? Why do many wives today refuse to do this?

b *For Adult Discussion:* What is the difference between being submissive and being inferior? Should the word "obey" be in the wedding vows for a woman? Give reasons why "obey" should be in the vows and why it should be left out.

Prayer Suggestions

Thank God that He has given us directions for getting along in the family. Ask Him to give us families and marriages which fit His directions. If you don't like God's plans, ask Him to help you accept how God has organized the family.

Day 6

Christian marriage is meant to be a lifelong relationship between one man and one woman, indissoluble except by death.

Read: Psalm 51:1-13

Do you know who wrote most of the Psalms in the Bible? It was a man named David. As a shepherd boy he used to play the harp and sing, and when he got older he lived in the palace and often sang for the king.

David had become very popular in the land. He was a hero because he had killed the giant Goliath and in this way made it possible for his country to win a war. But as David got more popular, King Saul got more jealous and tried to kill David with a spear. For a long time David had to hide, but when Saul died David became king himself.

Most people would agree that David was a good king. He was brave, fair, wealthy, and, most important, he worshiped God and encouraged the people to do the same. Like all of us, however, David was tempted to sin, and the Bible tells us about something he did which didn't please God at all.

It was late at night and David couldn't sleep because he was concerned about his armies who had gone away to war. As he walked on the balcony of his palace, David noticed a very beautiful woman taking a bath. He sent a messenger to find out who she was and then invited her to the palace. David was married and so was this woman, whose name was Bathsheba. They should not have been spending so much time together because soon they had a problem. They had begun to love each other, and when they discovered that Bathsheba was going to have a baby, they knew that they would be strongly criticized. Bathsheba's husband was away in the army and everyone would know that David was the baby's father.

David tried one or two plans to hide the fact that he and Bathsheba had been together, but when these didn't work, the king had another idea. He arranged to have Bathsheba's husband killed, and soon David and the woman got married.

A short time later, however, God sent a man to tell David that his sin was very wicked. "You have stolen a married woman," David was told, "and you have killed her husband." David was so sorry that he wrote a prayer asking God to forgive him. The prayer was what we read in our Bible reading today (Psalm 51:1-13).

Can you see what happens when married people turn away from their husband or wife and start loving someone else? This always creates problems. In David's life, for example, the baby that Bathsheba had became sick and died. Then there were family problems in the king's household. God forgave David and the king felt great sorrow for his sins, but the family troubles continued.

God does not want any of us to have family problems. That's why He has given us instructions for getting along with the people in our homes. The place to start, He says, is with the married couple. God expects them to stay married to each other until one of them dies. It takes work to get along like this, and sometimes it is easier to give up or to find somebody else to live with. But this isn't God's plan. When we don't take marriage seriously, family problems are sure to follow. The younger we are when we learn that, the better our lives will be.

Questions

a *For Family Discussion:* Why was God displeased with David? What happens when people keep breaking up their marriages and forming new ones? If God wants a man and woman to stay together for life, why do so many people not do this?

b *For Adult Discussion:* In our society is it really feasible to think that marriage can last for life? What can be done to build stronger marriages, including yours? Be specific and practical.

Prayer Suggestions

Thank God for what we have learned this week about Christian marriage. Thank Him too for revealing His plans to us. Ask Him to help all of us develop marriages which will last for life.

Part 3

Marriages That Crumble

Recently a magazine article told the story of a young college graduate named Connie. A brilliant student and the daughter of a New York physician, Connie was planning a career in mathematics, and she also looked forward to marriage and a family. On a vacation visit to the West Coast, however, Connie visited a commune, where she soon was attracted to the seemingly carefree lifestyle—and to a handsome, 25-year-old college dropout named Henry. Connie moved in with Henry, and the carefree lifestyle soon became careless sex. Nine months later, with a baby due in a matter of weeks, Connie and Henry went to see her family in the East. The contrast in age, dress, and lifestyle between the middle-class, middle-aged parents and the young lovers could not have been greater. "We don't need to marry," the young girl told her mother and father. "Marriage is outdated. It puts down women and it isn't necessary when you trust each other."

The story is a familiar one, and so is the attitude. People no longer take marriage seriously in our society. Sometimes they avoid it altogether and live in common-law arrangements. Sometimes they abuse it—with mate-swapping, extramarital affairs, trial relationships, or gay marriage. Or they may enter marriage with the attitude of trying it out until they either get bored or are convinced it won't work.

As a result of these attitudes, divorce has become increasingly common in our society. The statistics are difficult to interpret, but it is well-known that in some parts of our country there are as many divorces registered each year as there are marriages. For every legal breakup there may be other couples who stay together but are separated emotionally. Little wonder that whenever we attend a wedding these days it's easy to wonder, "Can this relationship survive?" With tongue in cheek, one man summed it up this way: "Sometimes I think I'd rather attend a Christian funeral than a Christian marriage—the outcome is more certain."

This is the focus for our thinking during the week ahead. What does the Bible say about divorce? What should be our attitude toward this subject? How should we treat divorced people? What should we teach our families about separation, divorce, and remarriage? These are difficult questions, but important ones for families to consider together.

We affirm the permanence of marriage as the intent of God. We believe that divorce is contrary to God's intention for marriage.

Read: Malachi 2:1, 2, 13-16

Men and boys have trouble understanding this, but girls really like to play with dolls! If we had boys in our house I suppose they would prefer trucks or basketballs, but little girls (and bigger ones too) seem to enjoy dolls. As you know, dolls (like children) come in all shapes and sizes. There are big dolls, little dolls, white dolls, black dolls, oriental dolls, Indian dolls, baby dolls, grown-up dolls, Barbie dolls, cuddly dolls, paper dolls, male dolls, female dolls, expensive dolls, 39¢ dolls, and dolls that cry, talk, crawl, wet their diapers, chew, drink, blink, and probably do other things that I haven't heard about yet. And of course there are also the stuffed animals, but these don't really count as dolls.

Sometimes I hear my children playing with their dolls, and this is an interesting learning experience for me. A few days ago, for example, I discovered that the dolls had been organized into a family. Apparently there was a husband who had some children from a marriage which had ended in divorce, and there was a wife, also divorced with several children of her own. These two adults with their children had decided to get married to form a new family.

Maybe I'm old-fashioned, but when I was small it never would have occurred to us to think of a family in this way. But something has happened to marriage in the last few years. Most couples can't seem to get along anymore, and it isn't hard to get a divorce if you really want one. As a result, more and more marriages are breaking up. Often children watch their parents fight, and then either their father or mother moves away. Then a stranger becomes a "new father" or a "new mother," who very often comes with more children to join the family.

Sometimes things are better then, especially if the old marriage made everybody miserable. But very often new problems arise, and this is hard on everybody, especially the children.

Today divorce has become very common, but did you notice in the Bible reading what God thinks about this? He hates divorce and has told His people to work at getting along, so that divorce will not be necessary.

Notice that God does not hate divorced people. He loves and cares for all of us, whether we are divorced or not. He wants us to be happy, but He knows that divorce is very painful and brings sadness into many lives. Very often divorce includes sin, and God wants that to be avoided. So He tells us of His hatred for something which is so unpleasant and against God's plan for His creatures.

The men that we read about in the Bible today were worshiping God but weren't being good to their wives. In fact, they were divorcing their wives because they saw women around who looked more attractive.

The same thing happens today. God wants us to stay married and work at getting along, but too many people grow tired of their mates and get interested in somebody else. Before long they begin forming new marriages like the doll families in our house.

Dolls, of course, are only toys. They don't feel hurt like real people do when there is divorce. Husbands and wives (and the children too) must work at solving their problems and staying together. Then we won't have to feel the real hurt that comes whenever there is divorce.

Questions

a *For Family Discussion:* What is divorce? Why do you suppose God hates divorce? If God hates divorce, why doesn't He hate divorced people?

b *For Adult Discussion:* Do you think there are times when divorce is necessary? When? Are such divorces approved by Biblical writers? If you are married, discuss this with your mate: "What are we doing to prevent a disintegration of our marriage? What should we be doing?" Be specific.

Prayer Suggestions

Thank God for telling us what He thinks about divorce. Ask Him to help married couples—especially the ones you know best—to avoid divorce. If you know couples or children involved in a divorce, ask God to help them through this difficult time in their lives.

Day 2

Divorce is a profound human tragedy leaving a legacy of anguish, bitterness, loneliness, a sense of failure, and a deep fear of close personal relations.

Read: Matthew 19:1-9

Have you ever watched sports on television and seen somebody lose? The TV pictures usually show the smiling winner, but think of the people who played very hard or worked very hard to get ready for the game, only to lose. Sometimes people cry when they lose, and there are probably many others who feel like crying but don't. Other people get angry when they lose, or sometimes they sulk.

We have some of the same sad feelings when we lose a friend. A couple of years ago a boy in our neighborhood was killed in an accident. The people on our street knew him; in fact he sometimes played ball on our front lawn. When he died it was hard for the neighborhood kids and for their parents. Someone important had gone out of their lives. If you have had a relative die or have said goodbye to a very good friend who is moving away, you know something about real sadness.

Divorce is a sad thing like this. Even when married life has had many problems, there is still loneliness and unhappiness when a marriage breaks up. It's like working at something for a long time and then failing. It's like seeing somebody go away, somebody you used to love very much and maybe still do love. Divorce hurts. It hurts the husband and wife, and it hurts the children too. And it also hurts the grandparents and sometimes the neighbors or friends.

One day Jesus was asked about this. He had just finished preaching and healing some sick people when some men asked, "Do you permit divorce?"

Jesus told them to read the Bible where it says that God planned for married couples to stay together for their whole lives.

"But," the men answered, "the Bible also says that God lets people get a divorce."

It's not because God wants it that way, Jesus said. It's because all people are sinful: married people, single people, and divorced people too. We have evil hearts and sometimes we disobey God. When one person in a marriage goes to love somebody else, for example, this is sin which sometimes leads to a divorce. Jesus wasn't saying that all divorce is wrong, but all divorce comes because we are all sinful people. Often we would rather do what is wrong than to do what God wants. Sooner or later this always leads to unhappiness—the kind of unhappiness that comes with divorce.

Questions

a *For Family Discussion:* Why does divorce make people feel sad or lonely? Can you think of some reasons why divorce is not a good idea? Is there ever a time when divorce is all right? (Parents: see Matthew 19:9 and explain it in simple language if necessary.)

b *For Adult Discussion:* Reread the sentence of the family affirmation that we are considering today. Is divorce always a "tragedy bringing anguish, bitterness, etc."? Give reasons for your answer. Reread Matthew 19:9. Does Jesus allow divorce? When?

Prayer Suggestions

Thank God for the good things that come with a happy marriage. Ask Him to help you, your friends, and your parents avoid divorce. Pray again for the divorced people you know.

Day 3

We regret the ease with which divorces are attained and believe that easy divorce and remarriage are among the factors contributing to the breakdown of family life. We believe that reconciliation is an alternative superior to divorce.

Read: 1 Corinthians 7:10-17

Have you ever noticed how children (and many adults as well) seem to enjoy nursery rhymes? The stories don't make much sense, but people like to repeat the rhymes about Little Miss Muffet, Little Jack Horner, Old King Cole, Mistress Mary, Little Boy Blue, Baa Baa Black Sheep, and Little Bo Peep. There's even one about a married couple; Jack Spratt must have been a thin man with a very plump wife! One of the most popular nursery rhymes concerns a fellow named Humpty Dumpty.

> Humpty Dumpty sat on a wall,
> Humpty Dumpty had a great fall.
> All the King's horses and all the King's men
> Couldn't put Humpty together again.

The reason for Humpty Dumpty's problem was, as everybody knows, that he was an egg and apparently one that hadn't been hard-boiled.

I wonder if some people think of their marriage as sort of a Humpty Dumpty thing. Perhaps the marriage isn't very strong in the first place, and when the marriage breaks up it seems useless to hope that anybody can get it back together again.

In the ancient city of Corinth, in Greece, the people were very sinful. They knew nothing about God, they lived to please themselves, and they certainly didn't take marriage very seriously. The Christians in Corinth found it difficult to obey God in the midst of so much sin, so the Apostle Paul wrote some letters to help the followers of Jesus live more holy lives.

Today we read part of one of these letters. Paul knew that many people were getting divorces then just like people do today, and he told the married people to do whatever they could to get along with each other. Try not to get a divorce, he said. It's hard for the husband and wife and often it is difficult for the children. Paul might have added, "If your marriage seems to be breaking up, try to get it back together again. Get other people to help. Maybe, like Humpty Dumpty, your marriage is cracked beyond repair, but if you can, it is better to patch things up than to let the marriage end in divorce."

Paul's advice is still true today. Very often people hurry to get divorces when they might be able to work out their problems and turn an unhappy marriage into a happy one. If either the husband or wife is a Christian, that person should try especially hard to get along with the non-Christian marriage partner.

But what if they still can't get along? Is it ever all right for Christians to get a divorce? A lot of people really don't know how to answer that question. The Bible seems to say that if a non-Christian wants to leave. this may be best. In times like that it may be more peaceful and better for everyone if the married couple separates and gets a divorce. It's not what God would really like, but it may be the only thing that can be done.

Questions

a *For Family Discussion:* If a couple is having problems getting along with each other, what should they do? When people all around us seem to be getting divorced, do you think it is possible for couples to really have a happy marriage? How can they do this? What can the children do to help their parents have a better marriage?

b *For Adult Discussion:* Look at the Affirmation statement. Do you think reconciliation is *always* superior to divorce? How can *you* keep your marriage or the marriages of your friends from heading toward a crack-up? What can your church do to prevent divorce? Be specific.

Prayer Suggestions

Thank God that He forgives us, cares for us, and helps us even when our marriages don't work out very well. Ask Him to show your family how to keep from breaking up.

Day 4

The remarriage of divorced persons is inconsistent with the plan of God for mankind, but in the opinion of some believers, it may be permitted because of divine grace and as a specific manifestation of the forgiveness and new beginnings offered to mankind by the Christian gospel.

Read: Romans 7:1-3

Has anybody ever asked you a question that you couldn't answer? This happens to parents all the time. Children love to ask questions like, "Why is the sky blue and not green? Why are porcupines prickly? Why do we call shutters shutters if they can't be shut? How can a brown cow eat green grass and make white milk?" Sometimes we can get answers to these questions in books, but some questions (like "How far is up?") just don't seem to have answers.

In our Bible reading today we are thinking about one of these hard questions: Is it all right for a divorced person to get married again? Of course the law of our country says this is all right. According to the law you can get divorced and married again as many times as you want.

But what does God say? We have learned that He hates divorce and doesn't like marriages to break up, but if a marriage does crack up, like Humpty Dumpty, do the divorced people have God's approval for getting married again to someone else?

This is a very hard question to answer because the Bible is not as clear about this as some of us would like. A few Christians say that getting married again after a divorce is *always* all right. Some Christians say that it is *never* all right for divorced people to remarry. Most Christians would probably say "sometimes it's all right and other times it isn't."

It's all right to get married again, for example, if your

divorced husband or wife dies. But what if you are divorced and your former husband or wife marries someone else? Are you free to get married? Many Christians would say yes, but this is a difficult problem—harder than the one about the prickly porcupines.

Maybe these hard questions can teach us some lessons, however. They teach us that some decisions in life are very difficult. Even Christians who love Jesus Christ and believe the Bible sometimes don't agree on things that are of great importance.

If you don't agree with another Christian about something, what should you do? Get mad? Argue? Call each other names? No! God expects us to respect one another, to show love for each other, and to try to talk about our differences. That can start in the family.

God also expects us to forgive. Do you know why? It's because God is always forgiving us and has told us to do the same with one another (Matthew 6:14, 15; 7:1, 2).

Does God say it's all right for divorced people to get married again? That's a hard question. A lot of people disagree on the answer. We must ask God to help us find the answer, and we must love those who don't answer the question like we do.

Questions

a *For Family Discussion:* Do you think it is all right for divorced people to get married again? (Parents: This is an opportunity for you to share the view on this issue that you want taught in the home.) How should we react to people who don't agree with our answers to this question? If a divorced person sins, do you think God forgives?

b *For Adult Discussion:* Reread the sentence of the Affirmation that applies today. Do you agree? Is remarriage after divorce ever permitted for Christians? If so, under what circumstances?

Prayer Suggestions

Thank God for the many things in the Bible that are clear and easy to understand. Ask Him to help us understand things that are not clear. Ask Him to help divorced Christians make the right decision about whether to get married again. Pray that we will learn to love and understand people who don't agree with us.

Day 5

The church must be a community of compassion, love, healing, and forgiveness for divorced, separated, and remarried persons.

Read: John 4:1-19, 26-30

Several years ago in the downtown section of a big city, a lady who was out shopping tripped and broke her leg. "Please help me," she pleaded with some of the people passing by, but nobody stopped.

"I was in a hurry," one man said when asked about it later. "I thought she was drunk," said another. "Everybody else was ignoring her, so I did too," replied somebody else.

It was only after she had lain on the sidewalk for 45 minutes that a taxi driver came along and took the lady to the hospital.

What do you think Jesus would have done if He had been walking along that street that day? I'm sure He would have helped the lady. He was always concerned about other people. He healed them, helped them, listened to them, forgave them, and taught them.

We see this in the Bible verses that we read today. About noon one day, Jesus stopped to rest near a well in a place called Samaria. The disciples had gone to town to get some lunch, but before they returned a woman came by to get water at the well, and Jesus asked for a drink. Today this doesn't seem like a strange request, but it was in the time of Jesus. Jesus was a Jew, and most Jews didn't get along very well with the people from Samaria. In fact, they often didn't talk to each other. In addition, Jesus was a Jewish teacher, a Rabbi, and in those days Rabbis never spoke to women in public. So the woman was surprised at what happened next. Jesus told her that He was the Messiah, the

Savior that the people had been awaiting for many years.

Jesus soon showed that He already knew something about this woman at the well. He knew that she had been married five times, and I think we can assume that at least some of these marriages must have ended in divorce. Also, at the time she met Jesus, the woman had been living with a man who was not her husband. Here was a lady whose marriages had not lasted and who even then was sinning by living with a man to whom she was not married. Even before they met, Jesus knew all about this woman, but notice how he treated her—with kindness and concern.

Did you know that this doesn't always happen in churches today? Very often Christians are unkind to divorced people. If someone is divorced he or she is criticized, is never invited to parties, is not allowed to work in the church, is not forgiven, and is hardly shown any love or kindness. That's about as cruel as walking by the lady who had fallen in the city with a broken leg. And to be unkind to another person is something that should never be done by a follower of Jesus.

In the past few days we have seen that God hates divorce. He wants couples to work at getting along, and He is not pleased with all the divorces and remarriages that take place today. But God also loves us even when we sin. He treats divorced people with kindness and shows that He cares and accepts them. He expects us to treat divorced people in the same way. It is sin for us to do otherwise.

By the way, do you know what happened to the divorced woman who met Jesus at the well? She became a Christian, and God used her to tell many others about the Messiah. God still uses divorced people today, and He loves them. He expects us to do the same.

Questions

a *For Family Discussion:* Why do you think divorced people are not treated kindly by others today? Is your family guilty of rejecting divorced people? Think about Jesus and the woman at the well. Is it possible to be a real follower of Jesus and not be willing to forgive people or help those in need?

b *For Adult Discussion:* Why do you think divorced people so often get treated as "second-class citizens" in the church? Is there any reason to deny divorced people full involvement (including leadership positions) in the church? Are you guilty of the tendency to forgive former swindlers, gamblers, and robbers—even encouraging them to give their testimony publicly— while you treat divorce as an unpardonable sin? What can your church do to act in accordance with the portion of the Affirmation statement we read today?

Prayer Suggestions

Thank God that He cares for, loves, heals, and is willing to forgive all people, including divorced people, and including you. Ask Him to help you, the members of your family, and the people in your church to be more compassionate toward divorced, separated, and remarried people.

Day 6

The Church must also attempt to prevent divorce by clearly and persistently setting forth the Biblical teachings on marriage and sex relations, and by providing a therapeutic community of believers.

Read: 2 Corinthians 6:11-18

I have noticed something interesting in our house lately: all of a sudden the children seem to know a lot about divorce. Do you know how they learned? They learned from talking with their friends at school. Many of these school friends come from homes where parents are divorced, and often these homes aren't very happy.

Wouldn't it be good if we could stop so much divorce in our country? Wouldn't it be great if more husbands and wives could get along better so that children would not live in houses where there is arguing all the time?

The place to start working on these problems is with God. He loves us and wants our homes to be happy. According to the Bible, if we ask God to come into our lives He lives inside each of us and is right there to help when family problems come along. But a lot of people never ask for His help, and instead they try to deal with their problems alone.

A second thing we can do is to make our homes like God wants them to be. We talked about that last week. The Bible has given some instructions for the husband, the wife, and the children. We get into trouble when we ignore God's instructions. Obedience to God's plan always makes life better at home.

Then, third, we can try to love each other. Love is more than a feeling. Love means doing something kind to each other and not saying words which hurt or start an argument. We need to show this love at home and to people in our church or neighborhood. It is also important to show a real love both to people with marriage problems and to their children. If we show that we care, others will be helped.

But there is one other thing. We should always be careful who we marry. It is hard for a Christian and a non-Christian to get along well with each other, even though this is sometimes possible.

Have you ever seen two horses pulling a wagon? They often run together and do a pretty good job. But what do you suppose would happen if we attached the wagon to a horse and a cow? There would be problems! For one thing, cows are slower than horses, and it is possible that one animal might be stronger than the other—or larger.

Something like this happens when a follower of Jesus gets married to someone who is not a part of God's family. The husband and wife are going in different directions because one is following Jesus but the other is not. One is trying to walk with God but the other is not.

You can save yourself a lot of problems if you marry someone who loves God like you do. This is what God intended as a way to be happily married without getting a divorce.

Questions

a *For Family Discussion:* How can we stop families from breaking up? Can you remember the four things mentioned in today's reading? Do *you* show kindness to other people in your family and neighborhood? Can you think of some thoughtful thing you have done today or yesterday? What kind thing could you do for someone in your family next week?

b *For Adult Discussion:* Reread 2 Corinthians 6:14. Can this apply to marriage? Is there any hope for harmony in a marriage where one person is a believer and the other is not? How can *you* fulfill the suggestion put forth in the sentence of the Affirmation statement that we read today? Try to be specific.

Prayer Suggestions

Thank God for His love to us and for the love we can have for each other. Ask Him to help us get along better in our homes. Ask Him to work in the minds of the unmarried people in the family so that if and when they marry, they will find another Christian.

Part 4

What to Do with the Kids

Children have been called "bundles from heaven," "blessings from God," and "the joy of life." They have also been called "problems," "the source of all frustrations," "brats," and a variety of other derogatory terms.

It isn't easy to raise children in our society today. Perhaps that's why there are so many books on child-rearing, and so many battered, mixed-up kids. To really be successful, parenting takes the wisdom of Solomon, the patience of Job, the dedication of Hannah, and the leadership skills of Moses. None of us has all of this, of course, so parents find themselves frustrated, confused, and impatient at the same time as they are amazed by a child's complexity, amused by childish antics, delighted by children's maturation, and warmed by a child's company and fellowship.

It surely is amazing that God entrusted the raising of children to the care of parents—rank amateurs who don't know how to do the job. When we finally learn how, our children have grown up and aren't interested in the acquired wisdom of their parents! But God didn't leave us to flounder completely. In the pages of Scripture He outlined what He expects of parents, what He wants for children, and how He guides us in child-rearing. These are important topics for children, parents, and nonparents alike. The future of our society rests on how we train children, but at least some writers have suggested that we aren't training them very well. This is the basis for our discussion this week: what do we do with the kids?

We affirm that children, natural and adopted, are a heritage from God, given in sacred trust. They are not to be abused or neglected. Children are not pawns of the Church, state, or parents.

Read: 1 Samuel 2:18-21, 26

Do you remember who Samuel was? He lived hundreds of years ago and was a man who loved God very much. He was a judge over the whole nation of Israel, and he spent his life trying to get people to obey God.

Samuel's mother was a woman named Hannah and his father's name was Elkanah. In those days if a husband and wife didn't have children, everybody wondered why and thought that God must be angry with the couple. So you can understand why Elkanah and especially Hannah were very sad, since for many years after their marriage they had no children. The Bible says that Hannah cried and cried about this and didn't even feel like eating.

One day Hannah went to the Temple to pray. "O Lord of heaven," she prayed, "if you will look down on my sorrow and answer my prayer and give me a son, then I will give him back to you, and he will be yours for his entire lifetime. . . ." And that is exactly what happened. Hannah had a baby boy and named him Samuel. He was a gift from God.

Have you ever thought about the fact that children are a gift from God? They are given to parents, and God expects that the parents will care for the children and teach them all they need to know in order to get along in the world.

Hannah and Elkanah took very good care of Samuel, but they also did something else. When Samuel was a very young boy, his parents took him to the Temple and left him there.

Now you may think that was cruel, but it wasn't. In her prayer Hannah had promised God that she would give Samuel back to the Lord. The young boy got good care in the Temple and good teaching. He became a helper to Eli, the priest, and as we read in the Bible today, everybody liked Samuel, including God. Hannah and Elkanah liked their son, too. Every year his mother would make him a new coat and the family would get together for a happy visit at the Temple.

Do you think it might have been sad for the parents and Samuel to be apart from each other? It probably was, but in another way there was gladness. The parents knew that Samuel was a gift from God who also belonged to God. When we give our children back to God, He puts a deep happiness in our lives so that we can thank Him even when things are not as pleasant as we would like. Sometimes missionaries must be separated from their children for a long time, and although this can be very sad, God can put a joy into everyone's life during the time apart.

In most homes today, God does not want parents and children to be away from each other. He wants parents to thank God for their children, to spend time with them, to teach them, and to treat them with kindness.

Have you ever borrowed a book from the library or something from a friend? How should we handle the things we borrow? We should handle them with special care because they belong to somebody else. The same is true with children. Maybe we ought to stamp a little sign someplace on newborn babies which says, "Handle with care! This child belongs to God."

Questions

a *For Family Discussion:* Do you think it was cruel for Samuel's parents to leave him at the Temple? Why? How can parents give their children to God today? What can children do to help?

b *For Adult Discussion:* In what ways can children be used as "pawns of the Church, state, or parents"? How can this be prevented? What is there about Hannah's attitude toward Samuel that would be a good example for parents today?

Prayer Suggestions

Let's thank God that He has put children into homes. Thank Him for your parents.

Day 2

Every child deserves to have a warm, caring relationship with a mother and father, the opportunity to develop a healthy self-esteem through loving parents, and the opportunity to be nurtured in an environment which models Christian behavior and values.

Read: Genesis 21:1-3, 8-20

In the Old Testament we read that Abraham had two sons: Ishmael, who was older, and Isaac. These boys had the same father but they didn't have the same mother, and this caused some problems.

Not long after Isaac was born the family had a big party, but Isaac's mother Sarah wasn't happy. When she saw that Isaac was being teased by his brother, she demanded that Abraham get rid of Ishmael, and this is exactly what he did.

Early one morning Abraham got up, prepared a lunch, got some water, and then sent Ishmael out into the desert with Hagar his mother. Soon the water was gone, and Hagar decided that she and Ishmael would probably die because they had nothing to eat or drink, no place to live, and nowhere to go. But God heard their cries. He gave them more water, took care of them, and protected them as Ishmael grew to become a man.

Did you know that God cares for families and watches over them? He also gives parents the job of raising children, and He wants homes to be places where the mother and father both love and care for the children together.

Many homes are not like this today. In some homes either the father or mother is gone and one parent has to raise the children alone. This is what Hagar had to do—take care of Ishmael without the help of a father. One-parent homes can be very good homes, but it isn't easy for one adult to be both a mother and a father.

Much worse, perhaps, are the homes where children are treated badly. In some families the children are beaten (that's worse than being spanked), yelled at, and neglected. I know one couple who didn't want their baby so they criticized him, complained about him, and hollered so much at him that he grew up feeling unloved and of no importance. Not long ago, another couple so disliked having a baby that they put the child in the garbage, where she was found the next day by the man who came to get the trash. Every year hundreds of children are beaten so badly by their parents that the children must be put in the hospital and sometimes even die.

Why do some parents beat their children, say bad things about them, or kick them out? That is a hard question to answer. It is easier to answer the question of what God wants for our homes. He wants the family members to love each other, to care for each other, and to say good things about each other. He wants parents to be like Jesus and to show by their actions what it means to be a Christian.

One thing Jesus does is to love us even when we are bad. He doesn't ignore our sin. He forgives us when we do something wrong, and He teaches us (sometimes using discipline) how to do what is right. That is what parents should do with their children.

Abraham probably provided a good home for his son Isaac, but the other son, Ishmael, was put out of the house. God cared for both of these children, but His real desire is that parents will not treat their children like Abraham treated Ishmael, but like Isaac was brought up—with a loving, caring mother and father.

Questions

a *For Family Discussion:* Was Abraham a good parent? Why? What kinds of parents does God want for children today? How is spanking a child different from beating a child until he or she must go to the hospital?

b *For Adult Discussion:* Why was Sarah so critical and rejecting of Hagar? Does this historical account have any modern applications? How do parents build self-esteem in children? Do you have an unwanted child in your home? Be honest. In what ways do your attitudes and actions influence this child adversely? How could your attitudes and actions change?

Prayer Suggestions

Thank God that He cares for children and families even when the families break up or the parents are cruel. Ask Him to bring more and more peace to your home. Pray for children who even today are in homes where they are unwanted or treated cruelly.

We believe that the roles of parents include providing for their children's growth (mentally, physically, spiritually, and socially) and teaching them from the Word of God in a spirit of Christian love and nurture.

Read: Luke 2:41-52

Nobody knows very much about the childhood of Jesus. We know about His birth in the manger of Bethlehem, we know about the time His parents took Him to the Temple a few days after He was born, and we know that the little family had to hurry to Egypt when the king decided to kill all the babies in the land. After King Herod died, the family came back to a town named Nazareth, and it was there that Jesus grew up.

During the days when Jesus was a boy, a very important highway ran through the town of Nazareth, and many times interesting travelers would stay in town overnight. Jesus probably saw many of these travelers, and He may even have talked with some of them. But most of His time was probably spent in school and in Joseph's workshop learning to be a carpenter.

Every year Joseph would leave the carpenter shop for a few days and travel with Mary to Jerusalem, where they would take part in a big religious celebration. Children didn't attend this until they were almost teenagers, but at the age of 12 they would journey to the celebration with their parents and join the crowds in the Temple.

The family of Jesus did not travel alone. In order to protect themselves from robbers, families in those days often traveled together in a large group. Usually the women would be together in one part of the group, the men would be together in another part, and the young people would be with their friends. At the end of the day, the families would all come together again.

It was only after they had traveled for a whole day on the journey home from the celebration that Mary and Joseph discovered that Jesus was not with them. Nobody had seen Him since leaving Jerusalem, and nobody knew where He was.

The next day Mary and Joseph hurried back to Jerusalem and looked all over for Jesus. When they found Him they must have been both relieved and surprised. Jesus, a 12-year-old boy, was sitting with all the leaders in the Temple, asking questions and discussing religion like a college graduate. Even Mary and Joseph didn't know what to make of that.

I wonder if Jesus visited with these leaders in the Temple when He went back to Jerusalem the following years. The Bible doesn't tell us! All it says is that Jesus went home with his parents and grew up.

According to the Bible, Jesus got bigger. He "grew in stature." That's not surprising, because healthy people grow a lot during the teenage years as their bodies become adult in size and shape.

It also says, however, that Jesus grew in wisdom. His mind was growing so that He could learn more facts, think more clearly, and discover how to solve problems.

Jesus also grew in His religious life. He was obedient to God and did things which pleased His heavenly Father. Certainly His parents taught Him from the Scriptures, and, like the other boys, He would have gone to the synagogue very often to learn about God from the rabbis there.

There is one other thing we know about Jesus. He was liked by the people around Him. He learned to get along with His friends and relatives, and did not fight with the neighborhood kids.

What happened to Jesus as He grew is what God wants for children today. They are to grow to have bodies that are as strong and healthy as possible, and minds that think clearly and know how to tell right from wrong. Then God wants us to be growing as Christians, learning to obey Him. Finally, He wants us to learn how to get along with people, including the people in our homes. Mary and Joseph helped Jesus to grow in these different ways, and even today God expects parents to help in the growth of their children and teenagers.

Questions

a *For Family Discussion:* In your family, how can the children grow 1) to have healthy bodies, 2) to have good minds, 3) to please God more, 4) to get along with others? How can parents help with the growth in these four areas?

b *For Adult Discussion:* Do we ever stop developing physically, intellectually, spiritually, and socially? How can adults keep growing in these areas? How can we help children to grow in these areas?

Prayer Suggestions

Thank God for families and churches where we all can learn. Ask Him to help parents and church teachers to do a better job in raising children. Ask Him to help the children in your family to develop healthy bodies, good minds, a deep respect and obedience for God, and the ability to get along well with others.

Day 4

Parents, together, are responsible to teach spiritual truth and other information by word of mouth and by example.

Read: Deuteronomy 6:1, 4-7

Recently a newspaper columnist asked her readers an interesting question: "If you had it all to do over again, would you have children?"

Ten thousand parents answered that question, and of those who wrote in, seven out of ten parents said, "No, I wouldn't have children if I had it to do all over again."

I wish they had asked me. My reply would have been "Yes! Yes! Yes!" I'm glad we have children in our home. Having them was not a mistake, even though children create problems. They are helpless when they are babies, and sometimes smelly and noisy. They spill things when they get older and are sometimes very stubborn. But they are fun, especially as they grow up, learn new things, and finally become independent adults.

Teaching children to grow up is a pretty important job, and sometimes it is surprising to me that God gave the job to parents who aren't always sure what they should be doing.

Think of teaching children about God, for example. How should that be done? Some parents just send their children to church and hope the job will get done that way, but that doesn't always work very well. For one thing, church services really don't last very long (you just *think* they last long!) and sometimes children don't learn the right things there. When some children were asked recently to tell what church was all about they gave some interesting answers:

—"Church is a place where you dress up and wear squeaky shoes."

—"Church is where my mom and dad make me go on Sunday."

—"At church they make you keep quiet while adults talk and talk and talk."

—"Church is a place which was fun when the kids sat on Jesus' knee under a tree, but it isn't fun anymore."

I'm sure all children don't feel like this. Many enjoy Sunday school and church and we learn a lot about God there. But if we are really going to learn about God, the teaching has to take place in more places than church.

Parents—mothers and fathers together—must teach their children about God. The parents can do this in two ways—by *talking* about God at home or wherever they are with the children, and by *showing* the children what it is like to really trust God.

Not long ago we had a little problem in our house. We were looking for a new house, and we finally found a place we liked. We were all set to buy the new place when the lady who owned the property did a sneaky thing. She raised the price and in some other ways made it impossible for us to buy the new home. We were all disappointed, but we discussed our feelings one night after dinner. "Why does God let her do these things?" somebody asked. "Shouldn't we hate her?" asked one of the children.

It was a good chance for us all to talk about what had happened and to pray about it as a family. Very soon we discovered that God had a better place for our family to live.

In the Bible reading today we read about God's commandments to His followers many years ago. "Parents," He said, "you must love God. You must think about His commandments. And you must teach them to your children when you are at home or out for a walk; at bedtime and the first thing in the morning."

He could have said, "Teach your children about God when things go wrong and when things go well; when you are in the car or when you are at a shopping center; when you are alone as a family or when you have guests."

Anytime is the time to think about God. Even now!

Questions

a *For Family Discussion:* Do you think church or Sunday school is the only place to learn about God? Is this family discussion time the only time to learn about God? Is it the best time? Where else can we learn about God? Can you think of times when you have talked about God as a family? Why don't you look for a chance to discuss or worship God sometime during the next 24 hours?

b *For Adult Discussion:* Do you look for opportunities to discuss spiritual things with the people who live in your home? What, if anything, is the value of this? Do you think such discussions can replace personal devotions or church worship? Can these discussions be good learning experiences, even for adults?

Prayer Suggestions

Thank God that we live in a country where we are free to talk freely about God. Ask Him to make the parents you know 1) become more obedient to God and 2) become better teachers about God. Pray that God will remind you of chances to talk about Him.

Day 5

They [parents] are to discipline in a firm, consistent, loving manner in the home.

Read: Hebrews 12:2, 5-11

Have you ever gone to the circus and wondered how the performers got to be so good in doing their acts? It looks so easy to swing on the trapeze, to walk on a little wire hanging in the air, to stand on your head on a bicycle, or to be a juggler; but when *we* try these things it's really pretty hard! Try to juggle four oranges sometime (or even three), and before long you're likely to have orange juice on your shoes! Circus acts are a lot harder than they look.

As we all know, it takes a lot of time and practice to develop a skill like juggling, but it also takes patience and something called discipline. According to the dictionary discipline means the same thing as training. The juggler trains himself (or herself) to juggle without dropping the balls. Tennis players have this training or discipline, and so do ice skaters, piano players, and singers.

Do you know who else needs discipline? Children. Discipline means that a person is corrected so that he or she can stop making mistakes and learn to do things better.

Let's assume a little child runs into a busy street but is pulled back to the sidewalk by a parent. The parent could have ignored the child and hoped that he or she would never wander into the street again, but that wouldn't be very loving. Neither would it be loving if the parent beat the child and hollered, "You're bad!"

It would be much better if the parent spoke sternly to the child and said firmly, "No! No! No!" Sometimes it may even be necessary to spank the child to teach a lesson. To be firm like this is not because the parent is angry; it's because the parent loves the child and wants to teach a very important lesson—children must not wander into the street. If the child is older, the parent might say something like this: "I don't want to hurt you, but I love you too much to let you get away with what you are doing. It will harm you in the end."

Parents must discipline because they love and want the best for their children, and the same is true with God. He disciplines us, His children. This teaches us what God wants us to know and helps to protect us from harm.

Let's go back to that little child who wandered into the road. If a mother just let the child walk in front of the cars, what would you think of that mother? I'd think she really didn't love her child very much. Perhaps the same is true of parents who don't discipline their children. If we really love our children, we discipline them, just like God loves and disciplines us who are His children. When we are disciplined by our parents we should be glad that we are learning from loving parents, even though it hurts.

Questions

a *For Family Discussion:* What is discipline? Why is discipline important? If discipline means that we are loved, why does it hurt?

b *For Adult Discussion:* What, if anything, is the difference between discipline and punishment? Is there a difference between discipline and nagging? What does the divine discipline described in Hebrews 12 teach us about parental discipline?

Prayer Suggestions

Thank God that He loves us enough to discipline us. Ask Him to help us appreciate discipline. Ask Him to help the parents in your house to discipline the children "in a firm, consistent, loving manner."

Day 6

The role of the child includes becoming an obedient learner who is being trained to become a mature adult able to exercise wise and responsible discernment in making decisions.

Read: Ephesians 6:1-4

Many years ago I was in the Navy. It was fun wearing a uniform, riding around the world on ships, and sometimes marching in parades. But there were things which weren't so much fun. One was that we were expected to obey our officers.

Think what it would have been like if each one of us decided to do what he wanted. Imagine the morning of a parade which was due to start at 9 o'clock. Suppose that three people came at 8:00 and decided to get the parade over early, so they started down Main Street on their own. At 9:00 most of the sailors appear, but suppose a few of them decide to go for coffee before the parade, others decide they want to march near the band, some decide they're too tired for a parade, and others think it would be nicer to join the crowds on Main Street to watch.

That would be a pretty stupid parade. To avoid such confusion our officers used to say, "Be here at 9 o'clock dressed properly, and we will all step off together when the band plays and the commanding officer orders 'quick march.' If you don't appear, you will be disciplined!" Without such obedience the military would collapse. And there's something even more important. When people learn obedience in a parade they will be ready to obey if they get into battle, where you could get killed if you don't obey. In the military, you have to obey.

But the same is true for Christians. God wants all of His children to obey. Parents are to obey God, they are to obey the Bible, and they must obey the law. If we don't obey, we get into trouble and sometimes we even get put into jail.

Children are to obey too! Very often kids don't like the part of the Bible which says, "Children, obey your parents," but parents think it's great! This, however, is one of the biggest problem verses in the Bible. Children often don't like to obey parents, and parents sometimes have trouble making them obey. That creates all kinds of difficulties!

So how do we learn to obey? We are taught to obey by our parents. The children, according to today's Bible reading, are expected to obey. To obey parents is the same as obeying God, because God has put parents in authority over children. When children obey parents they are pleasing God. They are learning how to become wise and happy adults who can make decisions on their own, and God even promises them a "long life, full of blessing." So God expects children to obey.

But God expects something else, too. He expects parents to help children obey. That's not easy, especially when the children refuse to cooperate. Parents must remember that children are people who have feelings, but the children must be taught to obey immediately—without a lot of coaxing and anger. If children don't obey they must be disciplined firmly but lovingly. The parents must give advice and help, so that children learn to do what they are told.

Some homes are run like the parade we talked about. Everybody does what he or she wants, and as a result there is confusion, no cooperation, and unhappiness. The children aren't prepared for the future, and life becomes difficult for them. So children, obey your parents! And parents, help them obey.

Questions

a *For Family Discussion:* Why should children obey their parents? How can parents help them obey?

b *For Adult Discussion:* How can we teach obedience in our homes today? What is the effect of our obedience? Do you think adult obedience to God and to the state is the one way to teach obedience to children? As an adult have you learned obedience?

Prayer Suggestions

Thank God that He has shown us the importance of obedience. Ask Him to help you obey Him and (if you are young) ask Him to help you obey your parents. Pray that God will teach the parents in your home how to help their children obey.

Part 5

Happiness Is a Warm Family

Do you remember the famous "Peanuts" cartoon showing Charlie Brown hugging Snoopy the dog? The caption read, "Happiness is a warm puppy." I'm not sure all parents would agree that happiness comes with a puppy (especially when the puppy is not house-trained!), but most of us realize that a lot of happiness does come from warm family relationships.

The problem is that a lot of families aren't very warm. Cold stares and "cold shoulders," dissension, disagreements, insensitivity, conflict, boredom, and lack of concern for each other all seem to characterize a number of families today. In many homes there may be intellectual agreement that "happiness is a warm family," but as the family members are well aware, what they actually have is nothing but a cold and sometimes feuding family.

The part of the Affirmation which we will discuss this week concerns family closeness—how we can bring our families closer together, cut down on family conflict, and at the same time let each family member develop his (or her) own interests if he wants to. That's how we develop warm families.

Day 1

Children are to honor their parents, to obey them as they would obey the Lord, and to care for their needs in old age. Each member of the Christian family has spiritual gifts which are to be discovered, developed, and used to glorify God and strengthen each other within the family.

Read: 1 Timothy 5:1-4, 8

My grandfather was an interesting man. He lived in our house when I was growing up, and when I was a boy he used to take me places—to the park, to the high bridge near our home, where we could see just about everything, and to the lake, where we would watch the pleasure boats leave and return with happy passengers.

My grandfather used funny words like "conundrum" and said silly little rhymes like, "Dicky dicky dout with your shirttail out; half a mile in and half a mile out."

When I was about 12 he had a stroke one night. He couldn't speak, couldn't walk, and never recognized any of us again. He spent the last weeks of his life in the hospital, and when he died I went to the first funeral I had ever attended. I didn't think boys were supposed to cry, so I waited until the funeral was over and I could go alone to my room at night. Then I cried!

When he was healthy, my grandfather used to tell me to treat old people kindly. "Remember," he would say, "you will be old someday too!"

When we think of families we often think of parents with little kids or teenagers. But older people are parts of families too, and the Bible talks about them.

"Don't speak sharply to an older man," it says; "treat older women as mothers . . . thinking only pure thoughts about them." Notice, however, that we are expected to take care of our relatives when they need help. If we don't care for our family members, the Bible says, it may be that we are not even Christians.

Sometimes it isn't easy to care for our relatives. God made us all different. He gave us different abilities, different personalities, and different interests. Sometimes, therefore, it's difficult to get along with the people in our families who are not like us. But the fact that we are not alike lets us help each other, and because of our differences we can even praise God in different ways.

When my grandfather was old, he liked to talk with kids like me. I was young and interested in things that didn't interest him, but we helped each other and we learned to get along.

Do you get along with your relatives—especially the older relatives like parents and grandparents? Do you care for them and help them? The Bible reading today says something very interesting: "Kindness should begin at home." God expects us to be kind and helpful to people in our own houses. And notice what else the Bible says about this kindness: "It pleases God very much."

My grandfather was kind to me and I hope I was kind to him. I also want to be kind to the members of my family. Do you?

Questions

a *For Family Discussion:* Why is it important to be kind to our relatives and to care for our parents when they get old? What have you done today that is kind to other people in your family? What kinds of things could you do tomorrow?

b *For Adult Discussion:* Reread verses 4 and 8 of 1 Timothy 5. Does this apply in a time when Medicare and the state provide so much for older relatives? What is the church's obligation to the elderly? What is your obligation to your older relatives?

Prayer Suggestions

Thank God for grandparents, parents, and older relatives. Ask God to help you be kind to the people in your family.

Day 2

We deeply regret the breakdown in family closeness and order, and we urge mothers and especially fathers to resume their God-ordained roles as leaders in the home.

Read: 1 Samuel 3:1-18

The story of Samuel and Eli has been told many times. The young boy in the Temple kept hearing his name called at night, and he thought the calls were coming from Eli the old priest. But it wasn't Eli who was calling Samuel; it was God, and God had a very interesting message.

"I am going to punish Eli and his family," God said to Samuel. "Eli has been a good priest but he hasn't been a good father. He has watched his sons sin and he hasn't done a thing about it."

Eli's sons, Hophni and Phinehas, used to steal from the people, and what was worse, they stole the offerings that had been brought for the Lord. Sometimes they committed great sins with the women who would come to worship God, and everyone knew what was going on. Eli heard about the sins of his sons, but about all he did was to say "It's awful—God won't be pleased!" Eli never disciplined his sons, and he didn't teach them to obey God.

So do you know what happened next? There was a big war and Eli's sons went off to battle, but even there they disobeyed God. In the middle of the battle the two sons of Eli died, and when Eli heard this he was so sad that he fell off his chair (the Bible says he was very old and fat), broke his neck, and died too.

God wants fathers and mothers to teach their children how to obey God and how to obey their parents. It is important for families to do things together, to learn together, to take vacations together, and to have fun as a family.

Besides reading this book, what does your family do together? The answer will depend on the size of your family, the age of your family members, and where your family lives. In our house we do things together (like working around the yard, going out to a restaurant for breakfast, visiting shopping centers and sometimes amusement parks or museums, going ice skating together, or taking trips as a family). Sometimes mom and dad go someplace alone, sometimes mom may go shopping with one of the children, and sometimes dad takes one of the kids out for the evening.

Most of all, we try to talk. In a kind and loving way we say what we are feeling and show an interest in each other's friends and what each family member does during the day. Sometimes we get mad at each other and say unkind things, but then we apologize and talk about our disagreements. All of this helps us to build closeness as a family—the kind of closeness that Eli's family never had.

Questions

a *For Family Discussion:* What does your family do to build closeness? What could the mother do to build closeness? What about the father? The children? What things have you done since yesterday to be kind to the members of your family?

b *For Adult Discussion:* There is a lot of talk today about "the breakdown in family closeness and order." What things push to create this breakdown in *your* family? How could the male and female leaders in your home "resume their God-ordained roles as leaders in the home"? Be specific.

Prayer Suggestions

Thank God for family closeness. Ask Him to draw your family closer together. Ask Him 1) to help your family talk more fully about your needs and feelings, and 2) to help the parents (especially men) accept their responsibilities as leaders in the home.

Day 3

We oppose the unhealthy influences which seek to exploit children through pornography, drug abuse, and unethical advertising. We are deeply concerned about the harmful effects of television, films, and printed news media. . . .

Read: Genesis 35:1-4

Do you know what an idol is? It is something we worship instead of God.

In some parts of the world idols are carved out of wood or stone, and people bow down before them at home or in a temple. These idols aren't very powerful. In fact, they don't have any power at all! They may have eyes or ears, but they can't see and neither can they hear. They have mouths which can't talk, noses which can't smell, arms which can't move, feet which are not able to move, and no brains at all!

It doesn't make any sense for people to worship lifeless idols when they can worship the living, powerful God. In fact, God has commanded us to worship Him and to get rid of idols (Exodus 20:3-5; 1 John 5:21). This is exactly what Jacob was trying to do in the part of the Bible which we read today. "Worship me," God had said, so Jacob told everybody in his family to destroy their idols and bury them underground beneath a big oak tree.

Where we live, people don't worship idols made of wood or stone anymore, but did you know that there can be modern idols of a different kind? What is the most important thing in the world to you? What do you think about more than anything else? The things that you mention as you answer these questions may very well be more important in your life than God is.

For some people television is the most important thing in life. For others, music or getting a lot of money or becoming famous or doing well at sports or having a lot of friends or any number of other things become most important. These things are modern idols if they pull us away from God and become more important than He is. These things can also harm our families and keep us from getting along with each other.

Consider television, for example. You probably enjoy watching it—most of us do—and there are some good programs for us to see. But TV programs can also do great harm, and this includes cartoons. To watch murders, fighting, lying, and stealing, for example, is to fill our minds with moral garbage, and this can cause great harm. Television tries to make us believe that people don't really need God, that marriage isn't important, that fighting is a good way to solve our problems, or that money and pleasure are the most important things in life.

Television, pleasant as it can be, may also become an idol in people's lives. Remember, anything which is more important to us than God is really an idol. Movies can also become idols, and so can books, magazines, clothes, friends, or sports. These things are not wrong in themselves, but they become wrong if they are more important to us than God.

The Bible tells us pretty clearly what to do about these idols. "Dear children," it says, "keep yourselves from idols . . . keep away from anything that might take God's place in your hearts" (1 John 5:21). Like Jacob, we must get rid of any idol which keeps us away from God.

Questions

a *For Family Discussion:* What is an idol? Do you have any idols in your life? Can your friends be like idols? What should we do about idols?

b *For Adult Discussion:* Reread the portion of the Affirmation statement that is being considered today. How do pornography, drug abuse, unethical advertising, television, films, and the printed news media exploit children and harm your family? What can *your* family do about these influences? Be specific. Is it possible that even "the family" can become an idol? How can we prevent this?

Prayer Suggestions

Thank God for warning us about idols. Ask Him to protect us from idols and to keep us close to Him.

Day 4

We oppose . . . the lack of discipline and poor adult example in home and school, and the breakdown of family unity and cohesion.

Read: Acts 5:1-11

Do you know what a phony is? It is someone who pretends to be something that he or she is not. Suppose, for example, somebody says "be kind to animals" but then hurts cats by pulling on their tails—this person is being a phony.

Ananias and Sapphira were phonies. As we read today, they sold some land, kept some of the money, and brought the rest as a gift to the church. It was then that Ananias showed that he was a phony. "It is important to give all of your money to the church," he must have said, "and that is what we are doing."

But Ananias was lying. He was a phony who pretended to do one thing (giving God all his money) but did something else (he kept some of the money for himself).

Now there was nothing wrong with Ananias and Sapphira keeping part of the money and bringing the rest to God. What was wrong was that they lied about what they did. They pretended to be giving everything but were really hiding part of the money. God wasn't pleased with their phoniness, and both Ananias and his wife died because of their sin.

I once knew a college student who was very upset because her father was a phony. "He always goes to church," the student said. "He works hard in the church, carries a big Bible, and likes everybody to think he is a fine Christian."

At home, however, this man wasn't very nice at all. He would scream at his wife, beat his children, and sometimes say very unkind things to his family. No wonder his family thought he was a phony. He said one thing in church— "I'm a fine Christian"—but his actions at home weren't very Christlike.

A lot of people today are phonies. They don't die because of their phoniness, like Ananias and Sapphira, but phoniness causes problems in their marriages, their families, and their own lives.

Most of us have lied at some time in our lives and then tried to hide our dishonesty. That's a very uncomfortable position to be in. There is a fear that we will be caught in our lying, and sometimes we tell more untruths to cover up our earlier lies. When we are dishonest like this, it makes us feel afraid inside, and then we have trouble getting along with others because we don't want them to know what we are really like.

Adults must learn to stop being phonies—to stop pretending to be something we are not. Teenagers and children must also stop being phonies. If we can be honest with each other in a loving way, we will be better Christians and will get along better in our families.

Questions

a *For Family Discussion:* What does it mean to be phony? Can you think of some examples of phoniness? How can we be less phony? How will this help our families?

b *For Adult Discussion:* How can adults provide a better example for the young people in our homes, churches, and society? How can *you* avoid being a poor adult example? Be specific. Does phoniness contribute to the breakdown in family unity and cohesion? How?

Prayer Suggestions

Thank God that He is always honest with us. Ask Him to help us to be less phony in our homes and churches. Pray that the adults in your home will be a better example for others, especially the children in the family.

We urge parents and schools to raise and teach children in a climate of mature love, respect, and discipline.

Read: 2 Timothy 1:1-5; 3:14-17

The Bible tells us a lot about the Apostle Paul. For example, he had a good education, he was very religious, and he hated Christians until one day he met Jesus on a road which led to a place called Damascus. Paul soon became a follower of Christ and told many people about the Lord. It was Paul who wrote many of the books in the New Testament, and Paul was also the first Christian who ever became a missionary. Of course it wasn't easy to follow Christ in those days (it never is). Paul was beaten, shipwrecked, often in danger of being hurt, and several times thrown into jail. But he kept on obeying God right up to the end of his life.

Paul's closest friend was a young man named Timothy, and in our Bible reading today we read what Paul wrote about his friend. Timothy was well-liked, he traveled on Paul's missionary journeys, and he took some trips of his own. Timothy was honest, godly, and a willing worker, and more than anything else he wanted to follow Jesus Christ.

Have you ever wondered how Timothy got to be like this? There were many other people in the Bible who claimed to be Christians, but they weren't very serious about their religion and they didn't pay much attention to it.

Maybe one reason for Timothy's love of God was the fact that as a boy Timothy had learned about the Bible in his home. His father may not have been a believer, but his mother (whose name was Eunice) and his grandmother (Lois) had told Timothy about the Bible, and he had become a very sincere Christian.

Today God expects both mothers and fathers to teach

their children about the Bible and to show them how to live a good Christian life. It takes time to teach these things, and sometimes parents don't want to bother doing this. But the kids aren't always interested in learning, either.

Do you suppose Timothy, Eunice, and Lois got bored as they studied the Bible? I think they did at times. Some parts of the Bible are not as exciting as others, and probably all of us get bored at times. But of course there is a lot in the Bible that *is* very interesting, and as Paul told Timothy in another letter, all of the Bible is well worth studying. To read God's Word helps us to become men and women of God who are ready and able to do good works for God, even as Timothy did. It is the job of teachers and parents to teach young people about the Bible even when nobody wants to be bothered.

Questions

a *For Family Discussion:* Do you get bored in reading the Bible? Why? How can your Bible reading and prayer times be less boring? How should parents train their children in spiritual things?

b *For Adult Discussion:* How can parents and schools "raise and teach children in a climate of mature love, respect, and discipline"? If you are parents, answer how *you* can raise and teach *your* children. According to 2 Timothy 3:16, the Bible "straightens us out and helps us to do what is right." How can we make this happen in our homes and lives?

Prayer Suggestions

Thank God that He has given us the Bible and that He has given us parents and teachers who can help children to grow spiritually. Ask Him to teach parents how to raise their children, and ask Him to help the children you know learn the Scriptures like Timothy did.

Day 6

We urge churches to give priority attention to the task of equipping parents to provide homes in which the spiritual, psychological, intellectual, and social development of children is of crucial importance.

Read: Exodus 2:1-10

Do you remember this true story about the baby Moses? The king of Egypt had become worried because there were too many Jewish babies being born in the land. "What if these babies, especially the boys, grow up and fight against me?" the king thought. "Or what if they become so many that they become very powerful and refuse to work as our slaves?"

The king was so worried about this that he ordered the soldiers to kill all the Jewish baby boys. "Throw them into the Nile River," he commanded.

But Moses' parents didn't want this to happen to their son, so they hid the baby in a little boat which floated in the river. One day the king's daughter found the baby and decided that she should raise him as her son. Moses' mother was hired to take care of the child, and the young boy grew up to become an honest man who was very much concerned about other people.

The Bible shows us clearly that Moses' parents cared for him very much. They must have protected him carefully, and they probably taught him about God too, because as a man Moses knew a lot about God.

This doesn't always happen in our day. In fact, some parents don't seem to care much for their children. Every year thousands of girls and boys are severely beaten by their parents, and sometimes these children even end up in hospitals. This is called "child abuse" and it is one of the biggest and saddest problems in our country.

Do you know something else which is sad? It is when parents who love their children nevertheless do not teach the children about God. We learn about God in church, of course, but such learning should also take place at home.

Raising children is not easy. It takes time, effort, money, work, and a lot of difficult decisions. Many married couples have decided that it is easier and better for them if they do not even have children, but other couples decide that they want to have babies. When these babies begin to grow up they are sometimes noisy, stubborn, and hard to handle. But they are also fun.

The parent's task is not to beat up the children or to ignore them. Parents are to care for their children, to teach them, and to bring them up in a way which pleases God. And the church has the task of helping parents with this task. When church people and parents can work together to teach children, the family is stronger and the young people can become the adults God wants them to be.

Questions

a *For Family Discussion:* Why do you think Moses' parents were good parents? Why do you think some parents beat their children? What can your church do to help parents teach their children?

b *For Adult Discussion:* Do you think the church can have an influence in the prevention of child abuse? How can the church help families like yours in the area of child-rearing? Be specific.

Prayer Suggestions

Thank God for parents who love their children and care for them. Ask Him to protect those children whose parents beat up their kids. Ask God to help your church teach parents how to do a better job at child-rearing.

Part 6

One-Person Families

What comes to mind when you hear the word "family"? For most of us we probably think of a husband and wife with one or more children. But, depending on our background and past experiences, we might also think of numerous relatives, including aunts, uncles, cousins, and grandparents. For some people the word "family" is linked with "good times together," but for others the family is only a group of people who seem to delight in criticism and arguments.

Few people seem to think about families as including widows, old men and women, divorced people, college students who are away at school, or unmarried people. Often people are separated from their larger families, and frequently they live alone or with a roommate who is not a relative. Churches, which should exist as families for God's children in a local community, sometimes ignore the unmarried, widowed, or divorced persons in their midst. Rather than finding a place of welcome and an opportunity for service within the church, these single people often feel unwelcome, especially when there are "family retreats," "sweetheart banquets," and "couples clubs."

This week we want to focus our attention on those people who live apart from their relatives. These are the people who form "one-person families." Such people are important to God, especially since many of them are part of God's family, and they should be important to all of us as well

Day 1

We agree that the single life is a valid lifestyle for many Christians and one to which some have been called by God. Singleness and celibacy are, for some persons, gifts from God preferable to marriage, and conducive to greater personal and spiritual development.

Read: 1 Corinthians 7:6-8, 26, 27, 38

When I was a little kid we used to have some interesting ideas about marriage. "When girls grow up they always want to get married," we used to say, "but when boys get bigger they are never interested in marriage." When I grew up, I found that these ideas weren't true at all. Men got married as well as women, even though there are a lot of people who stay single all their lives.

Did you know that single people can have some very special problems? Sometimes they are lonely or unhappy, but perhaps their biggest problem comes from other people who like to criticize or ignore them. "Why didn't they get married?" we sometimes ask ourselves about single people. "Couldn't they find anyone? Didn't anybody want them?" These are very cruel questions—questions which suggest that there must be something wrong with people who don't get married.

There are many reasons why people stay single. It is true that sometimes they can't find a mate. (For example, there are more women living today than men, so that means there aren't enough husbands for all the women who want one.) Sometimes the single person does not want to be tied down to a wife or husband. In Christians, however, there is another reason for singleness. God wants some people to remain unmarried. Consider the Apostle Paul, for example. He never got married, and some of his best friends were apparently single too.

In the Bible today we read Paul's statement that marriage is fine, but singleness is better. Why would we read something like that in the Bible? Do you suppose Paul didn't like women or couldn't find a wife? No. Paul knew that for some people, like himself, it is best to stay single so they can serve God better. If you are married, Paul said, you get very busy caring for your family, so that there isn't much time left to work for God (1 Corinthians 7:32-38). Single people usually don't have families to worry about, so they are better able to do Christian work.

The next time you talk to single adults, think about the fact that God may not want them to get married. Singleness is not something to criticize, for single people are often used by God in a special way. After all, even Jesus never got married!

Questions

a *For Family Discussion:* What people do you know who are single adults? What are some good things about being single? What are bad points about singleness? Do you criticize single people because they are not married? Why is this criticism wrong?

b *For Adult Discussion:* Read 1 Corinthians 7:32-38. Does this imply that the married person's family should take precedence over his or her Christian work? What is your attitude to singles? What should it be?

Prayer Suggestions

Thank God for the people you know who are single. Ask God to make them happy and useful in working for Him, whether they ever get married or not.

Many other single persons desire to marry but find no suitable mate for reasons beyond their control. We agree that the local church is intended to be the family of all God's people.

Read: 2 Timothy 4:3-8

When the Apostle Paul was a very old man, he wrote a letter to his young friend Timothy. Paul was in jail (because the authorities weren't pleased about his preaching the gospel) and he knew that very soon he might be killed. "I won't be around very much longer," Paul wrote in his letter. "Very soon I will be on my way to heaven." Paul had been a very sincere and obedient Christian who obeyed God. Now, since Paul was unable to work much longer, he was telling Timothy to keep up the job of telling others about Jesus.

If we had time to read all of Paul's letter to Timothy, we would discover something else: Paul was lonely. "Please come as soon as you can," he wrote. "Bring my coat and some books, but especially try to get here yourself before winter." As you know, Paul wasn't married. He didn't have a wife or children to be with him in his old age. And so he turned to other Christians—to people like Timothy. They became Paul's "family" and were especially important to him as he grew older and was by himself.

When I was growing up, I always looked forward to the time when it would be possible for me to travel. To go overseas and see faraway countries was something I had always wanted to do. Wouldn't it be great, I thought, to meet people, see sights, visit museums, and live thousands of miles from home? Finally the day came for my first long visit to Europe. The trip across the Atlantic was a lot of fun, but when I got to my little room in London, I suddenly felt very lonely. There were people all around—several million of them—but I didn't know anyone, and nobody in all of Europe cared about me or even knew my name. It was a very lonely time.

Very soon I made a decision. "Either I will sit here feeling sorry for myself all year," I thought, "or else I will go out and get to know some people."

But where do you find friends when you are alone in a strange place? For me there could be only one answer—in church.

Now I'd like to say that I found a nice church where everyone was so friendly that my loneliness disappeared. But I didn't. I had to find friends someplace else. The churches I visited didn't contain very many friendly people, and when holidays like Christmas came, I found that everyone was so busy in family activities that single people like me got pretty much left alone.

Has it ever occurred to you that your church could really be a big family of Christians? Of course there are smaller families within the church, but all the people in all these families are really part of a larger family of God's people. This church family includes children, their parents, and married couples who have no children. The church family also includes single people, old people whose wives or husbands have died, college students who are away from home, and other visitors, who might be lonely or looking for friends—like I was in London and like Paul was during his days in jail.

Your church should be a family for all of God's people, but especially for those people who are lonely, away from home, or not part of a family in your city or neighborhood. This was what God intended.

Questions

a *For Family Discussion:* Where did Paul, who had no family, find his friends? Do you have friends in the church? Does your family have an interest in old people or single people who don't have families of their own? Do you ever have these people into your home for holidays or for dinner? Could you?

b *For Adult Discussion:* When Paul wrote 2 Timothy, he was single, elderly, poor, of low status, and probably not very healthy. Would a person like this be welcome in your church? Would he or she ever be invited to your home? Be honest. What is your attitude and the attitude of your family toward single people? How could it be changed?

Prayer Suggestions

Thank God that as Christians we are all members of God's family. Pray for the single people you know. Pray for your church and your family, asking God to make you more concerned about the singles in your midst.

Day 3

We urge churches, individuals, and families to be sensitive to the needs of the single, divorced, and widowed persons in their fellowship and to help them develop a personal ministry and to establish meaningful relationships within the church family.

Read: 1 Corinthians 7:32-38

Can you think of people in the Bible who never got married? Try to think of some names.

Probably some of you are thinking of Mary, Martha, and Lazarus. They were, you might remember, a little family of two sisters and their brother who lived in a place called Bethany. Jesus liked to visit these three people, and He spent a lot of His spare time in their home. Once when Lazarus got sick, Mary and Martha sent a message for Jesus to come, but it wasn't until after Lazarus was dead and buried that Jesus arrived in Bethany. Then a wonderful thing happened—Jesus raised Lazarus from the dead! Many people praised God for this miracle, and the two sisters had their brother back with them for a while longer.

There was something special about Mary, Martha, and Lazarus—something which is special about single people who are alive today. Because they don't have families, single people are free to serve God in important ways. That's why our Bible reading today says that people who don't marry can often do a lot of good work in the church.

When I was single, I once went to a church where I met a lot of unmarried people. Before long I was attending their church meetings all the time, and the next year I was elected president of the single adult group. We all became very busy in the church, our group got larger, and God worked among us to help us grow as Christians. During that time I was probably doing more useful things in the local church than at any time since.

After being in that single adult group for two years, something wonderful happened—I got married! But I have never forgotten those years when a group of single people worked together so well in that church.

God wants single people to be busy doing His work. Unmarried people (including children, teenagers, young adults, or older singles), divorced persons, and those who are widowed can be doing a lot of useful things for Jesus Christ—just like Mary, Martha, and Lazarus did. The only trouble is that married people sometimes don't accept single people very well. That's very sad, especially when you remember that the greatest Person who ever lived, the one who served God better than anyone else, never had a wife or children.

Questions

a *For Family Discussion:* Think of some single, divorced, or widowed people in your church or family. Decide on what your family can do to help them. How are you going to *do* what you have decided?

b *For Adult Discussion:* Are single, divorced, and widowed people encouraged to take an active role in the life of your church? What are they doing? If they are not active, can you think why? Honestly now, do you harbor any prejudice against single, widowed, or divorced people? What can you do to change this? Be specific.

Prayer Suggestions

Thank God that He fully accepts unmarried people and welcomes them into His family. Ask Him to help the single people you know (including yourself?) to be more accepted and useful in your church.

Day 4

We affirm that widows and widowers are to be respected, honored, and accepted fully as equals in the body of believers.

Read: 1 Timothy 5:1-6, 16

Have you ever visited a foreign country? It can be a very pleasant experience (although sometimes it's unpleasant), and often when we travel we learn a lot about how people live in other parts of the world.

I remember, for example, the first time I visited India. It was a fascinating country, but how different from the place where I lived, and how surprised I was to see people sleeping in the streets (because they didn't have houses), riding in carriages pulled by oxen, getting water at the village wells, eating spicy foods that most North Americans would never like, and getting caught in the same kinds of traffic jams that people experience in Chicago, Paris, or Tokyo!

If you've traveled to other countries you may also have noticed that foreign people sometimes treat their old people differently than we do. In some parts of the world (like China, for instance), old people are honored because of their wisdom and experience. When an old person gets sick, the family rushes to help, and the old person feels a great sense of love.

That doesn't always happen in our country. We don't leave old people out in the cold to die, like some primitive tribes used to do, but we sometimes leave them alone in nursing homes, forget to visit them, and spend very little time in caring for them.

Perhaps this was happening many years ago when the Apostle Paul wrote the words which we read in the Bible today. We read these verses several weeks ago, but it is good to look at them again because they tell us how to care for the old people who are in our families. We read·

> Don't speak to them in an unkind way,
> Treat them with respect
>   [do you know how we can do this?],
> Think good thoughts about them.
> Take care of your parents as they grow older.

Sometimes this isn't easy to do. Did you know that even many adults have trouble taking care of their older parents and knowing how to treat them kindly? We have the same problem in the church—meeting the needs of older people, making them feel welcome, and listening to their opinions even when these seem outdated.

I have a friend, now over 80 years old, who lives in Switzerland and has some interesting thoughts about old people. "We old people," he says, "are very much like teenagers. We don't have much money, we have trouble finding jobs, we sometimes lose our friends, and at times we feel unwanted. Maybe," my friend has said, "maybe teenagers and old people could get together to help one another."

That's a good idea. In fact, children, teenagers, young adults, the middle-aged, and the elderly should all be trying to understand, help, and get along with each other. This is especially true in our families. That's what the Bible tells us to do.

Questions

a *For Family Discussion:* What is your opinion of old people? Be honest—do you really like them? How can we get along better with people who are older than we are (like our parents and grandparents)? What can you do within the next 24 hours to show kindness to someone who is older than you?

b *For Adult Discussion:* How, in specific practical ways, can we respect, honor, and fully accept older people—especially those who are widows and widowers? Are you doing what you should to care for the elderly members of your family?

Prayer Suggestions

Thank God for the older members of your family. Ask Him to protect and help them. Pray that you will be more tolerant of old people, more kind, and more willing to help those who are older.

Day 5

We are greatly disturbed by the dishonor and difficulties experienced by the aged and widowed in our society.

Read: Psalm 71:1-12, 17, 18

Today let's do something different. Let's stop right now and ask ourselves a question: What kinds of problems do old people face? You might want to write down your answers on a piece of paper, but whether you write them or not, try to think of the problems of being old.

What is interesting about all of this is that someday many of us will be old, and the problems we have been thinking about might very well become our own problems. Probably you thought of such things as:

—the loneliness which comes when the family moves away and/or one's mate dies.

—the pain of being sick or of discovering that one's body is wearing out.

—the problem of realizing that old people aren't liked much in our country and that often they feel pretty useless.

—the knowing that your children are too busy or not interested enough to care for you.

—the lack of money which comes when you can't work but sometimes have high medical bills.

—the boredom that comes when you don't have very much to do.

—the thought that death may be very near. This can be frightening, especially for people who know nothing about Jesus Christ and about eternal life.

Of course we shouldn't assume that all old people are miserable or that life for senior citizens is always a drag. Many people enjoy their old age, and it is fun to be around them. But for others old age is pretty unpleasant, and this should concern those of us who are younger.

The Bible reading today was apparently written by a very old man. Afraid that he would be forgotten in his old age, the man prayed that God would protect him and help with the problems of growing old.

But God never forgets old people, just as He never forgets the young. I wonder, however, if He wants people like you and I to be the ones who meet the needs of the elderly. He wants us to look after our older parents—and it is likely that our children will care for us just like we care for our parents.

When we pray for something, God often answers by sending another person who can help. Perhaps God wants to use *you* to answer the prayer of some older person— perhaps someone in your family—who is crying out, "Don't forsake me now when my strength is failing . . . O God . . . come quickly! Help!"

Questions

a *For Family Discussion:* Do you think God wants younger people to help the aged? Within the past 24 hours what have you done to help or be kind to an older person? What should you have done?

b *For Adult Discussion:* In Psalm 55:22 we are told to cast our burdens on the Lord, who in turn promises to sustain us. How do you react to the suggestion that God might sustain people by using concerned, helping Christians? Are you really willing to be used as a "sustainer" and helper of others?

Prayer Suggestions

Thank God that He lets some of us live to experience a happy old age. Ask Him to help those who are old and bothered by problems. Pray that He will show you how to help old people, and ask Him to give you an attitude of love and concern for the aged.

Day 6

Family members are to honor and care for the widowed, especially those who are elderly. The church also has responsibility to nurture and, where appropriate, to minister to the elderly, neglected, lonely, and needy in a spirit of Christian acceptance and concern.

Read: Titus 2:1-5

Have you ever thought what you might be like when *you* are old? Think of yourself as an old lady or an old man. What will you look like? What kind of person might you be?

I remember an old lady whose name was Mrs. McGowen. She lived in a little house with her grown-up son, who was drunk most of the time, and with a husband who didn't treat her very well. Life must have been very hard for Mrs. McGowen, but she never seemed to complain. She had a rocking chair on her front porch, and the neighborhood kids used to come by to visit and talk with her on warm summer evenings. Mrs. McGowen was a pleasant, friendly, gracious old lady.

Upstairs over Mrs. McGowen's house there lived a man who wasn't even old yet—he was still middle-aged. I don't know if I ever knew his name, but there is one thing about him that I do remember: he was an old crab. He screamed at the kids, complained about everything, and gave the impression that he didn't like anybody—not even nice Mrs. McGowen.

Now why do you think Mrs. McGowen was such a fine old lady whom everyone liked, while her neighbor was so unpleasant? Might it be that Mrs. McGowen was once a pleasant *young* lady, and that the man was crabby even when he was younger? People who are friendly, pleasant, and interested in others when they are young tend to be this way when they are old. People who are unfriendly complainers when they are young get even more unpleasant as they grow older.

The time to start being pleasant to people is *now*, and perhaps the place to start is with the old people you know. Many of them are lonely, forgotten by their families, unappreciated, and unwanted. As Christians it is our job to speak kindly to these people and to respect them, even if they are crabby like Mrs. McGowen's upstairs neighbor.

Our family once lived next door to an old people's home, where every afternoon when the weather was good the old people would come outside to walk or sit in the sun. Our children were very young then, but they used to visit these old people and talk to them. We soon discovered that older men and women liked little children, and our children in turn grew fond of the people who lived in the home. Sometimes just talking to old people, or writing them a letter, can make their lives a lot happier.

I used to talk a lot with Mrs. McGowen, and I think she liked that. She also showed me that even when old people are lonely and sad, they can still be pleasant and friendly. I want to be kind when I get older, so I guess I'd better be kind right now, both to old people and to those who are younger. Otherwise I might end up like Mrs. McGowen's complaining, crabby neighbor. What about you?

Questions

a *For Family Discussion:* Why are some old people crabby while others are pleasant and friendly? Do you realize that complaining in a sour manner can cause other people to criticize Christianity (look again at Titus 5:5)? Do you think *you* might be crabby when you are old? Why?

b *For Adult Discussion:* How could your church more effectively meet the needs of older people in your family, church, or community? How can you change to be more kind to others, including the elderly?

Prayer Suggestions

Thank God that He loves and accepts old people, whether they are pleasant or not. Ask Him to help *you* to 1) respect and be kind to old people and to 2) be the kind of young person who will be gracious in old age.

Part 7

One Plus One

We don't have to be very scholarly to realize that one plus one equals two. That's about the first thing we learn in school.

When it comes to the issue of human sexuality, however, the mathematics sometimes differ. According to the Bible, a husband and wife become *one* flesh. This is especially apparent during times of sexual intercourse, when one plus one equals one. Sex, however, is also God's way of reproduction, so we know that one plus one can equal three, four or more.

When God made us male and female, He knew all about hormones, sexual temptations, fantasies, and both the enjoyment and abuse of sex. But during the course of human history, something has gone terribly wrong with the sexuality which God created. At a time when sexual immorality was much less prevalent than it is now, the late C. S. Lewis wrote about our modern perversion of God's beautiful gift of sex:

> You can get a large audience together for a strip-tease act—that is, to watch a girl undress on the stage. Now suppose you come to a country where you could fill a

theatre by simply bringing a covered plate on the stage and then slowly lifting the cover so as to let everyone see, just before the lights went out, that it contained a mutton chop or a bit of bacon, would you not think that in that country something had gone wrong with its appetite for food? And would not any one who had grown up in a different world think there was something equally queer about the state of the sex instinct among us?"

In our deliberations this week we want to deal with this misuse of the sex instinct, but we want to do more. We want to talk about sex as something which was created by God to be expressed and enjoyed according to the divine plan. Sex, as we shall see, is honorable and consistent with personal holiness.

Please note: Before discussing it with their families, parents may wish to look over the second and third days' reading. These deal with the details of sexual intercourse.

"C.S. Lewis, *Mere Christianity* (New York: Macmillan, 1960), pp. 89-90.

Day 1

The human body and the capacity for sexual relationship, enjoyment, and reproduction are God's gifts to be received in an attitude of thanksgiving, wonder, and joyful worship.

Read: Psalm 139:1, 13-18

I remember the first time I went to see a really big circus. It was during my days as a high school student, and our class was on a trip to New York City. One evening we went down to Madison Square Garden, where the circus people were performing, and after the show we mingled with the crowds who had wandered backstage to get a closer look at the animals. A lot of the circus performers were there too, but I can remember only one of them. He was a little man, probably less than three feet tall, who was part of something they called the freak show. The man was friendly, told us a little bit about circus life, and even gave each of us an autographed picture of himself.

There was one thing about this man, however, that I never asked: "How does it feel to have such a little body and to be called a freak?" I wonder if he was happy about having a body which was so much different from that of other people.

Most people, even those of us who would never fit into a freak show, aren't completely happy with the way our bodies are made. Some people don't like the shape of their face, for example, or the size of their nose or chin, or their height, or the color of their skin. Older people sometimes dislike their wrinkles, baldness, or gray hair, and some people wish they were male instead of female or female instead of male.

What is interesting about our Bible reading today is the fact that God made our bodies. He gave us brains to think, eyes to see, ears to hear, legs to walk, hands to feel, and mouths to eat and talk. This human body is a wonderful, complex thing which began as just a tiny seed which formed in the darkness of a mother's womb. Even before any person saw our bodies, God saw them. He knew whether we would be male or female and normal in health or diseased in some way. He knew about freaks, and He was well aware of our big noses, ears which stick out, and other things about our bodies which we may not like. Not only did God see us before we were born, but He made us, and He still cares about us and our bodies every day.

Has it ever occurred to you that God could have made us different than we are? He could have made us to be all one sex, for example, but He didn't. He gave male bodies to some of us and female bodies to others—and He wants us to be thankful even for our sex organs. They are part of the world which God made, and our bodies are meant to be cared for and received with thanks, even if we aren't completely satisfied with what we have been given.

Questions

a *For Family Discussion:* Did you realize that God knows everything about us? Does that make you feel sad, happy, or both? Why? Are there things about our bodies that we don't like? Does the Bible reading today say anything about this?

b *For Adult Discussion:* What should be our attitude if we dislike some feature of our bodies? How do *you* react to the fact that God knows each of us intimately? Does Psalm 139:23, 24 have a sobering effect on you? Why?

Prayer Suggestions

Thank God for the way He made human bodies, including ours. Ask Him to help us take care of our bodies and be thankful for them. Pray that we won't criticize or make fun of other people whose bodies may not be very beautiful.

Day 2

We rejoice that God created male and female as sexual beings, and we affirm that sexual intercourse within marriage is good, desirable, honorable, and consistent with personal holiness.

Read: 1 Corinthians 6:19, 20; 7:3-5

Several years ago, I went one afternoon to visit the place where there once stood an ancient city known as Corinth. Although the old buildings now lie in ruins, in Bible times Corinth was a mighty port in the country of Greece. The people there had a lot of money, and the city was a center for the worship of pagan gods. There were temples there (some of the ruins can still be seen), and Corinth was known as a medical center where sick people could come to get treatment for their diseases.

There was something else about Corinth which people still remember about the city—the people who lived there were very wicked. Most of them knew nothing about God and weren't concerned about being holy people. Within the city, however, there was a little group of Christians, and the Apostle Paul wrote at least two letters to them.

In the Bible reading today we read from one of these letters. In it, Paul tells people what to do with their bodies. "If you are a Christian," he says, "you don't own your body—God does." He lives in your body, and if you are married He expects you to give your body to your husband or wife.

When He created us, God made it possible for husbands and wives to give their bodies to each other in a beautiful, loving, and very exciting way. It is wonderful to consider how a man's penis can get big and so stiff that it can glide into that opening in the woman known as the vagina. At times like this a couple are very close to each other, and as they stay in this position and liquid semen flows from the male into the female, the couple feels a very pleasant sensation. This act of sexual intercourse was designed by God to be something very beautiful, good, and pleasant. And it very often is just that, because that was what God intended. It is part of His plan for married couples.

As with all good things, however, some people have taken what God created and ruined it. They may refuse to have intercourse with their husband or wife, they think about their own pleasure, and they aren't very interested in whether the other person is having good feelings. Sometimes they decide that the sex that God created is dirty. They make unpleasant joking remarks about sexual intercourse, or they have sexual intercourse with a variety of people, even though God has told us to have intercourse only with our husband or wife (Hebrews 13:4). All of this makes God sad, because people who break His rules about sexual intercourse find sooner or later that they have sadness and problems.

Sex is not something to be ashamed of or laughed at. It is something beautiful, which God created to be enjoyed. And it is something for which we can thank God, unlike those people in Corinth (and many like them today) for whom sexual intercourse became a selfish act which is not the beautiful thing which God intended.

Questions

a *For Family Discussion:* Who owns your body? How can we treat our bodies in ways which please God? Can someone explain what is meant by sexual intercourse? Why is this only for married couples?

b *For Adult Discussion:* Notice in 1 Corinthians 7:3-5 that sex should satisfy both the male and the female. Is there ever a time when this need not be so? How would you answer the question, "Why is sexual intercourse only for married couples?" Does Hebrews 13:4 give an answer? (Note: "Adultery" means sex outside marriage.)

Prayer Suggestions

Let's thank God that He 1) made our bodies male and female, 2) lets married people have sexual intercourse, and 3) tells us how to live holy lives, even with our bodies. Pray that we will obey His rules for our bodies.

Day 3

Parents are to convey . . . attitudes [about sex] to children, along with providing factual information. Parents and churches have a God-assigned responsibility to provide moral guidance by word and by example so that God's gift of sex will be used in ways honoring Jesus Christ.

Read: 1 Thessalonians 4:1-8

Do you know what is one of the most beautiful things I have ever seen in my life? It was the birth of one of my daughters. Like the doctors and nurses in the room, I put on a green cap, a long gown, some cloth covers over my feet, and a mask over my face before marching into the room where my child was about to be born. My wife, who for several years had worked in a hospital helping doctors to deliver babies, was now lying on a table, getting the experience of being a patient for a change.

When the doctor pulled the baby out from between my wife's legs I saw a naked little creature who was covered with blood and a slimy fluid, but who was screaming to let us all know that she had indeed arrived.

My daughter is much older now, and she looks forward to the time someday when she will have a child of her own. When that happens and I become a grandfather, we probably will all marvel again at the complex little bodies which are born every day.

These babies would not come, of course, if it were not for sexual intercourse. When the father's penis is in the mother's vagina, a large number of little seeds flow from the male into the female. If one of these little seeds meets a tiny egg in the female, a child starts to develop who will be born—as my daughter was—nine months later.

When something is so wonderful as this is, isn't it sad that many parents never tell their children about it? And

149

isn't it sad that many teenagers and adults have intercourse with someone to whom they are not married, even though God has told us that this will bring a lot of unhappiness? And isn't it too bad that people make jokes about sex and think thoughts which God doesn't want them to think?

Sex is a gift from our heavenly Father, just like children, who also come from Him. Parents need to teach their children about this, and so should the church. The Bible says a lot about sex. It tells us how to live as males and females and how to use our bodies as God intended. This is God's plan, and it is the best for us. We can start now to treat our bodies in ways which please God, even if we are very young.

Questions

a *For Family Discussion:* Do you have questions about the way in which babies are formed and born or about how we feel or act sexually? Now would be a good time to discuss these questions as a family.

b *For Adult Discussion:* In what ways can sex be used in ways honoring Jesus Christ? How can parents and the church provide moral guidance and factual information for young people?

Prayer Suggestions

Thank God for the way in which babies grow and are born Ask Him to help your family think good thoughts about sex. Pray that there will be no misunderstandings about sexual intercourse, desirable sexual behavior, and childbirth in your family.

Day 4

We deplore distorted, unbiblical, and sinful sexual atti-
tudes and practices, both within and outside marriage,
which contribute to the breakdown of the family.

Read: 1 Corinthians 6:13-18

When I was young I always enjoyed Halloween. In our
neighborhood we did the usual "trick-or-treating," but in
addition there used to be a big community party for everybody, even the adults. The high school band would march
through town, the parents would line the streets, and the
kids would walk behind the band so everyone could see
their costumes. Part of the streets were blocked off, and it
was there that everyone would have cider and donuts while
we watched a magician or some other kind of entertainment. One year at this party I even won a prize. I was
dressed as a clown, and the judges decided that it was one
of the best costumes around.

Have you ever noticed how something as fun as Halloween can become harmful? Every year some children in
our country find razor blades hidden in their taffy apples or
harmful drugs tucked in the candy. How can some people
be so cruel that they want to hurt little children like this?
Have you ever wondered why people in this world enjoy
taking things which can be pleasant (like Halloween) and
misusing them?

There are many ways in which people take good things
and destroy or misuse them. God gave us a beautiful world
in which to live, but we destroy its beauty by leaving pop
bottles, beer cans, and paper strewn in the parks, by clog-
ging up the air with smoke from factories and burning
leaves, and by carelessly leaving campfires which burn
down acres and acres of trees. God has given us drugs to
make us better when we are sick, but many people misuse

151

drugs, taking what they don't need and using drugs for a lot of reasons other than to get well. Then think of the car. Automobiles can provide comfortable transportation, but some people misuse their cars—to speed away from stoplights, to drive recklessly, and to get away when they commit a crime.

Another thing that people misuse is sex. God made us male and female. He wanted husbands and wives to enjoy each other's bodies and to get very close to each other. But we have taken something very beautiful—the husband-wife closeness—and made it into something which is selfish and harmful. Instead of keeping their bodies for their husband or wife, many people (including teenagers) have shared their bodies with other people. Rather than covering our nudity as God commanded, we have paraded our nude bodies in public. Instead of thinking about things which please God, we have let our minds think about wrong sexual acts which God has told us not to think about. When we disobey God's plan for our bodies we have misery, sadness, and discouragement. None of this helps us, and neither does it make our families better.

Our bodies belong to Christ—that's what the Bible reading was about today. In fact, if we are Christians, God lives in our bodies. And if our bodies are really the place where God lives, shouldn't our bodies be kept clean, healthy, and as beautiful as possible? God will help us to do this. He has given us the power to think thoughts which please Him and to act in ways which obey His perfect plan for our lives.

Questions

a *For Family Discussion:* According to the Bible reading today, God owns our bodies and His Holy Spirit lives there. Since this is true, how should we take care of our bodies? What things should we *not* do with our bodies?

b *For Adult Discussion:* "Sexual sin is never right," we read today. Why not? In what ways might sex contribute to the breakdown of *your* family? Can this be prevented?

Prayer Suggestions

Thank God that He gave us our bodies and lives within us. Ask Him to help us keep our bodies and minds clean and honoring to Him.

Day 5

We resolve to resist the moral decline in our society, to teach that sex is to be enjoyed with mutual respect and fulfillment within marriage.

Read: 1 Timothy 4:1-5

Even people who don't have much of an interest in history know of the terrible suffering which took place during the Second World War. Thousands of people lost their homes, their lives, their families, their money, and for a while their freedom. Many were hurt in bombing or injured by gunfire, and even today there are thousands of people all over the world who are still crippled or scarred because of the war which took place many years ago.

When the war was all over, a doctor from Austria named Viktor Frankl wrote a book to tell how he had spent the war years in a prisoner-of-war camp. Although he was a physician, Dr. Frankl was forced to dig ditches, and every day he watched as his friends in the prison camp would be marched off to the big furnaces where thousands and thousands of men, women, and children were burned to death. The doctor's whole family died like this, and often he must have thought, "Will the soldiers kill me next?"

During this time Dr. Frankl lived in a little building which was cold and uncomfortable, but one night he peeked out through a crack in the wall to see the sunset. It was especially beautiful, and Dr. Frankl thought, "They can take everything away from me, but they can't take the beauty of the world."

We need to remember that everything which God created is good, including the earth on which we live, the air we breathe, the sunsets we enjoy, the food we can eat, and the bodies in which we live. These bodies are sexual, and that is good too.

God wanted us to enjoy sex completely, so He gave us rules to make sex really good. Sometimes it is hard to follow these rules, but there are two things to help us. First, we can ask God to keep our bodies from breaking God's perfect plans for sex. Second, we can think thoughts about sex which please God. Listening to songs which tell about impure sex, looking at pictures of people without clothes, reading sexy books or magazines, and thinking thoughts which disagree with God's view of sex—all of this is harmful. And all of this makes sex less pleasant than God intended it to be.

There are also people today who don't want to talk about our sexual bodies because they think such talk is dirty. Other people talk and joke too much about our bodies and especially about sexual intercourse. Both of these ideas are wrong. Our male and female bodies were made by God and are good. We should learn about our bodies, thank God for them, and ask Him to help us use our bodies in a way which makes God happy. He is happy and pleased when we are thankful for our male and female bodies, and willing to have sexual intercourse only with our husband or wife.

Questions

a *For Family Discussion:* The Bible teaches that in our times some people will teach things (including things about sex) that do not please Christ. What are some of these teachings? What are some correct teachings about sex and the use of our bodies?

b *For Adult Discussion:* How can we resist the moral decline in our society? Be specific. Are there ways to teach that sex is to be enjoyed?

Prayer Suggestions

Today let's pray about the attitudes toward sex in our society. Thank God that everything which He made is good. Ask Him to help you—and your family—to have the right kind of thinking about sex.

Day 6

[We resolve] to proclaim that ultimate control results from Christian maturation, which is brought about by the power of the Holy Spirit through the fellowship of the faithful and through happy, useful service to Christ.

Read: Acts 2:1-4, 40-47

What kind of church do you attend? When I was growing up we went to a big church. It didn't have 3000 or more members, like some churches today, but it had a big choir, lots of people, and even a church orchestra with violins, trombones, and other instruments.

Later, when I was a university student, I went to a much smaller church. There wasn't any orchestra or even an organ—just an old piano which most of the time was out of tune. We didn't have benches in that church, but just folding chairs which we squeezed into a room so small that we were really crowded if 35 or 40 people came to worship.

Another time our whole family attended a house church for a while. We met with a small group of Christians in the living room of a home, where the adults sat around in a circle drinking coffee and the kids sprawled on the floor.

I don't think they drank coffee in the churches we read about in the Bible, but the first Christians did meet in homes. Every day they went to the Temple for a big worship service, and then they met in homes in small groups, where they shared everything they had with each other.

There is a famous psychologist who once wrote that the best thing about the first Christians was that they met together in small groups. Certainly meeting together and sharing together is important for Christians, but two other things are also very important.

First, there is the fact that the early Christians served Christ. They didn't just sit around listening to a preacher (although they did that and learned from these sermons). They did things for other people. They were busy helping the needy, learning about Jesus, praying, and doing what they believed Jesus wanted them to do.

There was one other thing that made the early church powerful. The early church was effective because the Holy Spirit was there. He came to live in the lives of each Christian, teaching them and keeping them from sin.

In our day, whether we attend a big church, a small church, or even a house church, we can have the same exciting Christianity that the first Christians had. Suppose, for example, that Satan tempts you to sin, as he surely will. What can we do about it? Do we have any way to keep from sinning?

The early Christians had the answer, one which still applies to us today: we can ask the Holy Spirit to keep us from sinning, and we can rest assured that He will do so. We can make friends with other believers, getting close to them and praying with them. Then we can get busy doing things for others and for Christ. This is a plan to keep us from falling into sin, especially sexual sin. It's also a plan which will work in your church like it did in the first church many centuries ago.

Questions

a *For Family Discussion:* How is the best way for us to avoid sinning? Do you know how the Holy Spirit helps us and works in our lives? (See John 14:15-17).

b *For Adult Discussion:* Read 1 Corinthians 10:13. What does this say about sexual temptations? Can family members help each other with problems in this area, or must we turn for help to people outside the home?

Prayer Suggestions

Thank God for His Holy Spirit, who gives us the power to avoid and overcome sin. Thank Him for the friendship we can have with other Christians and for the chance to serve Him. Ask Him to give us the power to avoid sin. Pray that we can get closer to other Christians in a loving and sharing way.

Part 8

Zero Population Growth

Several years ago many of us finally woke up to realize what the experts had been telling us for years: the world's population is increasing too fast—faster than we can produce food to feed everybody. Suddenly, at least in North America, there was an interest in Zero Population Growth, or ZPG, as it was most often called. We were told that it was unpatriotic and, some said, morally wrong for any couple to have more than two children.

There are, of course, several ways to restrict population growth. Not having sexual intercourse is one way, and so is abortion, a topic which we will discuss later.

In the pages which follow we will consider birth control, but let's begin with a look at homosexuality. Although these are diverse issues, homosexuality and birth control both restrict population growth and both are of concern to families. Homosexuality has become widely accepted in our culture, and so has the use of birth-control methods by unmarried young people as well as by married adults. Now it is relatively easy to obtain contraceptives even in schools or through coin-operated machines in public washrooms. Families sometimes avoid discussion of these issues, but since they raise important moral issues and affect every one of us in one way or another, the place to discuss them is at home (and in the church).

We affirm that sexual unions between persons of the same sex are unbiblical and sinful, a perversion of the divine plan of the Creator. We oppose attempts by such homosexual unions to form unisex families through adoption or foster-parenthood of children.

Read: 1 Timothy 1:1-14

The Bible reading today is the first part of a letter that the Apostle Paul wrote to Timothy. In Bible times, letters were written differently than they are today. Instead of starting with "Dear Timothy," the letter begins with the words "From Paul . . . To Timothy" and then we read the message.

In his letter to Timothy, Paul said he was concerned about the fact that so many people were coming into the church and teaching ideas which were wrong. Before he became a Christian, Paul used to do the same thing. He didn't know much about Christ (in fact, he believed that Christians should be hunted down and mistreated), and he taught that people could gain God's favor only if they lived good lives and obeyed a lot of laws. In writing to Timothy, Paul pointed out that even in the church there were teachers who told lies, taught foolish ideas, and said things to confuse the Christians.

Did you know that the same thing is happening today? There are people in our churches, even pastors, who don't teach what the Bible says. They say, for example, that Jesus isn't God's Son, that the Bible is not God's Word, and that marriage isn't all that important. Another idea that some churches teach is that sex is not just for a male and female together.

There are many people in our country who feel more attracted to people of the same sex than to people of the opposite sex. Some men, for example, want to get married to other men and then adopt children. In the same way there are women who desire to marry other women and then adopt children together. A lot of people—even church people—say that this is all right, but the Bible teaches differently.

There is nothing wrong with people of the same sex being good friends or living together as roommates. But when two people of the same sex get involved with each other's bodies in a very close way, this is sinful, according to the Bible (Leviticus 18:22; 20:13; Romans 1:27; 1 Corinthians 6:9). God never intended men to marry men or women to marry women, nor did God plan for people of the same sex to have a sexual involvement with each other. Such a closeness with people of the same sex is called homosexuality, and it is something which goes completely against what God's Word teaches. It is also something which Paul wrote about in his first letter to Timothy (1:10).

Do you think that God hates homosexuals? No! God loves all of us, but He hates the sin in our lives. And just as God forgives our sins, He forgives homosexuals for their sin. Paul wasn't a homosexual, but, like you and I, he was a sinner who disobeyed God until God taught him to be obedient. Then Paul became a messenger who told people about God and wrote letters like the one we read today.

Questions

a *For Family Discussion:* What does God think about sin? What does He think about sinners? Is it wrong for people to want to marry someone of the same sex? Why? Is homosexuality part of God's perfect plan for us? (Parents note: this may be a good time to alert children—without frightening them—about the possibility of ventures from homosexual adults.)

b *For Adult Discussion:* In view of the current widespread acceptance of homosexuality, can we really hold the position that homosexuality is wrong? (In discussing this, look up the Scripture verses mentioned in the above paragraphs.) Does 1 John 1:9 have any relevance to homosexuality?

Prayer Suggestions

Thank God that we have the Bible which can keep us from untrue beliefs and ideas. Thank Him that He gave us a plan for using our bodies in ways which please Him and are best for us. Pray for people who are homosexuals and ask God to help them change.

Day 2

While we acknowledge that the Bible teaches homo-sexuality to be sinful, we recognize that a homosexual orientation can be the result of having been sinned against. We oppose the unjust and unkind treatment given to homo-sexuals by individuals, society, and the Church, and we urge the Church as the Body of Christ to accept such individuals as needing understanding, forgiveness, encouragement, and spiritual support.

Read: Matthew 18:1-6, 10-11

Can you think of anybody who is really great? Perhaps a lot of us would say that the greatest people alive today are leaders in the government, stars from the entertainment world, church leaders, scientists, or maybe people who are successful in business or sports.

When Jesus was asked about this, however, He told the disciples that in heaven the greatest people would be those who were like children—trusting, wanting to be obedient, and not trying to be "big shots." Another time Jesus said that in order to be really great we must be servants, doing things for other people instead of criticizing or looking down on them (Matthew 20:25-27).

Many of us seem to enjoy looking down on other people. We criticize the kids at school, are jealous of those who can do things better than we can, gossip about divorced people, and are unkind to others whom we don't like. Sometimes this attitude is shown toward homosexuals. "They're queer," we say, and sometimes we don't even want them to worship in our church.

It is important to remember some things about homo-sexual people. First, while some people try to marry others of the same sex and want to share their bodies with same-sex persons, there are others—many others—who might secretly like to do this but don't. Even married people with children sometimes secretly feel more love to someone of the same sex than to their own husband or wife. It is possible, therefore, to think homosexual thoughts and feel homosexual urges without doing homosexual acts. (Read that last sentence again to be sure everyone understands.)

Second, we should remember that nobody really knows why some people tend to be homosexual while others are not. Sometimes people have homosexual thoughts and feelings even though they wish they didn't. These people may have learned to feel this way through no fault of their own. This still doesn't make it right, any more than lying or stealing is okay just because a young person learned how to lie or steal without being caught.

It is important, then, for us to treat homosexuals like we would treat people who are not homosexuals. We should accept them, show concern for them, and help them to realize that God forgives them and can help them to change. Homosexuality is a sin, but we must not look down on homosexuals any more than we would look down on other sinners—including the little children we read about today, and including ourselves. These are the kinds of people Jesus loves—so much so that He came to die so we won't have to pay for our sins. But remember, He expects us to ask Him to forgive us our sins and then to stop sinning, so we can live lives that are pleasing to Him.

Questions

a *For Family Discussion:* The Bible says that homosexuality is sinful. Does this mean that we should be unkind to homosexuals? Why or why not? How does God
treat sinners like us?

b *For Adult Discussion:* What is your attitude toward
homosexuality? Do you see a difference between overt
homosexual behavior and secret homosexual urges? Is
one less wrong than the other? Can *you* really accept
homosexuals as individuals "needing understanding,
forgiveness, encouragement, and spiritual support"?

Prayer Suggestions

Thank God that He loves all of us, even when we sin. Ask
Him to keep us from sinning and pray that we will be willing to accept and love other people, even when they sin.

Day 3

We pledge ourselves to minister to those who are homosexually oriented in order to help them to change their lifestyle in a manner which brings glory to God.

Read: 2 Corinthians 5:16, 17, 21

Many centuries ago, the people in the land of Israel decided that they would like to have a king. God didn't think this was necessary because *He* was their leader, but the people kept asking, so finally God agreed. The new king was a man named Saul. He was a very handsome man—the most handsome man in all the land—and he was taller than anybody else in Israel. But King Saul disobeyed God. He did some foolish things, and finally God decided to make another man king.

One day God came to Samuel the prophet and told him to go and get the new king. As he left home Samuel didn't know who the king would be, but God had said that the king lived near Bethlehem and that his father's name was Jesse. When Samuel arrived he met one of Jesse's sons and decided, "Surely this must be God's choice." But God had an important lesson for Samuel to learn.

"Don't judge by a man's face or height," God said. "I don't make decisions the way you do! Men judge by outward appearance, but I look at a man's thoughts and intentions" (1 Samuel 16:7). God had already chosen a young boy named David to be king when he grew up.

A lot of us make the mistake that Samuel made. We look at people's outsides—their height, their dress, their age, their mannerisms—because we can't see how they really are on the inside. Sometimes people are not very good-looking on the outside but are kind, loving, and beautiful on the inside. The Apostle Paul was like that. He wasn't very handsome and he probably had bad eyesight, but he was a brand new person inside whose life was content and happy even when he was thrown in jail. Then there are people who appear to be peaceful, happy, and kind on the outside, but inside they are confused, unhappy, and sometimes very angry. King Saul was like that—a fine-looking man on the outside, but discouraged and unhappy within.

What are you like on the outside, and what are you like within? If you are unhappy inside, it makes sense to tell someone else about this so that he or she can help you feel better and solve your problems. And what if other people tell you *they* are unhappy inside? Our job as Christians is to listen carefully, help as much as we can, and pray for the person with the problems within. I think this is what Paul had in mind when he wrote that we should "share each other's troubles and problems"; "When God's children are in need, you be the one to help them out"; "When others are happy, be happy with them. If they are sad, share their sorrow" (Galatians 6:2; Romans 12:13, 15).

These past few days we have been talking about people who are or tend to be homosexuals. Sometimes these people are very unhappy inside, and God knows that. He looks on the inside. He pours His goodness into us, and He wants us to help unhappy people change so that their whole lives are able to praise God. Isn't it great that God uses people to help each other? Maybe He will use you to help someone else change to become the kind of person God wants us all to be!

Questions

a *For Family Discussion:* What did Samuel learn when he went to find the new king? Did you realize that God knows all about your thoughts and feelings inside? Why would it be good to share some or all of these inner thoughts and feelings with others?

b *For Adult Discussion:* Do you agree that a person who is a Christian, "a brand new person inside," could still have problems—even a problem with homosexuality? (Does Matthew 10:16-18, 23-25, 34-36 help with your answer?) In what practical ways can we "minister to those who are homosexually oriented"? What should a person in your family (perhaps even *you*) do if he or she has homosexual tendencies?

Prayer Suggestions

Begin by thanking God that He knows and understands our inner thoughts and feelings even though others do not. Ask Him to help us with our inner problems. Pray that we might be willing 1) to share our problems with people who love us and 2) to help other people when *they* share.

Day 4

We acknowledge that Christians differ in their views on birth control, and we respect these differences in the light of Scripture's almost total silence on this subject.

Read: Matthew 20:17-21, 24-29

Did you know that Christians, even good Christians who love Jesus very much, sometimes disagree with each other?

This happened once when Jesus was on His way to Jerusalem. He was talking about His crucifixion when two of His disciples, James and John, came with their mother to ask a favor. "When we get to heaven," they asked, "can we sit closest to you?"

This was a selfish request, and it gave Jesus a chance to explain that the greatest people in heaven would be those who are servants on earth. But the request of James and John did something else—it made the other disciples angry. Can you imagine that? The disciples of Jesus disagreed, perhaps even argued, with each other.

Something like this happened again many years later, long after Jesus had gone back to heaven. Peter, who was another disciple, was trying to please some Jewish leaders, so he said some things that were clearly wrong. The Apostle Paul disagreed with Peter and said so in front of many people. (You can read about this in Galatians 2:11-16). Once again two sincere Christians were disagreeing.

This happens all the time today. Christians disagree over such things as who they will vote for, which church is best, what some parts of the Bible mean, or how we should tell people about Jesus. When the Bible is clear on a subject we don't have to disagree. It is pretty clear, for example, that Jesus wants all of us to be kind to each other and willing to serve one another. But other questions are harder to answer, and that's when we have most of our disagreements.

Consider, for example, the matter of "birth control." Sometimes a husband and wife want to enjoy sexual intercourse but they don't want to have children. Young couples, for example, may want to finish school or save some money before having children. Older couples may decide that they don't want any more children or can't afford any more. Some couples decide that they never want children, but the husband and wife still like to show their love by having sexual intercourse.

To let them have intercourse without having unwanted children, many couples use some things called "contraceptives" or "birth-control methods." Some women, for example, take a pill which will prevent a child from developing, or perhaps a man will cover his penis with a little rubber bag so that the semen goes into the bag and does not enter the woman's body.

Is it all right for a husband and wife to use these things to keep them from having babies? The Bible doesn't say anything about this, and so some Christians disagree with each other about this. Some say, "Birth control is wrong," while others think it is fine if both the man and woman agree that they do not want any more children. Here is a modern issue where Christians disagree.

How should Christians handle disagreements? It doesn't make any sense to argue or fight. A much better solution is to look for answers in the Bible. This is what Paul did when he showed that Peter was wrong. If the Bible says nothing about the cause of our disagreements (as is true with the issue of birth control), then Christians should discuss their different opinions openly, but not be critical or unkind toward those who disagree.

Questions

a *For Family Discussion:* What are some things that you disagree about in your family? How do you handle your disagreements? How *should* they be handled?

b *For Adult Discussion:* What are the pros and cons of a couple using birth-control methods? What is your attitude toward other persons who may disagree with your thinking on this matter? What should be your attitude?

Prayer Suggestions

Thank God that He gives us sound minds which can think and even disagree. Pray that we will be able to know God's truth, even on matters like birth control. Ask God to help us respect other Christians with whom we may disagree.

God, at the time of creation, commanded mankind to be fruitful and multiply, and we rejoice in the birth of children as a heritage and gift from God.

Read: Psalm 127

Do you remember the story of the town of Babel? (See Genesis 11:1-9). It all happened thousands of years ago when some people decided to build a big tower which would reach high into the sky and stand as a monument to man's glory. The people worked hard to build their tower, but God confused their speech and scattered them all over the world because they were so proud of themselves.

Many years later, the psalmist wrote (in the psalm we read today) that man's work is useless unless God is helping us. God knows about our plans, our buildings, and our interests. He wants us to work hard, but not so hard that there is no time for rest.

God is also interested in our families. He gives us children, He cares about them as they grow up, and He tells us in the Bible that children are valuable people. When Adam and Eve first came into the world, God told them to have a lot of children so that the earth would be populated.

If children are so valuable, why is it that men and women often use birth-control methods to keep the size of their families small? Sometimes people who are not married use birth-control methods so they can have sexual intercourse without having to worry about babies. This is a wrong use of contraceptives. If the couple had a baby, everyone would know that they had sinned by having intercourse when they are not married. So birth-control methods are used by some people to help hide their sin.

But what about couples who are married and are free to have sexual intercourse? Why would they want to prevent themselves from having a lot of children, especially when the Bible says that children are a desirable gift from God?

There are many reasons for not having a lot of children. Can you think of some? Perhaps you thought of the fact that children cost a lot of money, and it makes sense to keep the family size small enough so the parents can pay for clothes, food, and education. Having a lot of children can also be hard on the mother's health, and if there are too many kids around, at times the noise can drive everybody crazy.

God, who knows all about us and everything about our lives, can help us to decide how many children to have. For some couples it is good to have a lot of children, while for others it may be better to have a few, or one, or even none at all. Whenever children do come, however, they should be received with thanksgiving, since they are a gift from God.

Questions

a *For Family Discussion:* What does the Bible mean when it says, "Unless the Lord builds a house, the builder's work is useless"? Can you explain what is meant by "birth control"? When is this all right for Christians?

b *For Adult Discussion:* If children are a gift from God, and mankind has been commanded to "be fruitful and multiply," is birth control really acceptable for Christians? How should young people be taught about birth-control methods and contraceptive devices?

Prayer Suggestions

Begin today by thanking God that He cares about our work and our families. Ask Him to help married couples decide when and if they should limit their family size through the use of birth-control methods.

Day 6

We are deeply concerned about the realities of overpopulation, world hunger, and the harmful effects that overpopulation can have on the environment and on individual families. We encourage Christian couples to limit the size of their families in a way that is not at variance with Biblical teaching and to keep family size to the number of children that can be nourished and taught effectively.

Read: James 2:14-17, 26

Have you ever been in a desert? Even if you haven't, you know that the desert is very hot. Not much grows there, and it is easy to get thirsty, especially during the day when the sun is shining.

Now let's suppose that you are driving across the desert some day (riding in an air-conditioned car) and you see a man lying by the side of the road. "I'm very hot," he says as you stop the car, "and I need some food and especially something cool to drink."

How do you think the man would react if all you did was to say, "Well, sir, I hope you can find a McDonald's to get a hamburger and Coke. Goodbye and God bless you"? Not only would this be stupid, but it would be cruel and unchristian. If we are followers of Christ, we are told to help people in need, even if this takes our time or costs us money.

There are millions of people in the world today who are starving. They have nothing to eat and their little children are dying from hunger. They don't use birth-control methods, so they keep having children who are hungry like their brothers, sisters, parents, and other relatives.

These people need food, but what do many Christians in our country say? "I hope they find something to eat. I'm too busy to worry about their problems. God bless them!"

Surely God isn't very pleased with us when we react like this. Of course *we* have pleanty to eat—so much that many of us eat too much and are overweight. But because the hungry people of the world are far away from us, it is easy to forget them.

There are some things we can do for these people, however. We can pray for the hungry children in the world and for the adults with whom they live. We can limit the size of our own families so we don't add too much to the world's population. (There are already more people in the world than we can feed.) Then we can learn more about the needs of the hungry and send money to people who can buy food and take it to those parts of the world where there is nothing to eat.°

Once I talked about this with a small group of Christians who were meeting in a home. "We don't want to hear about hungry people overseas," somebody said. "It's hard enough to feed my own family." I don't think our God is pleased with that attitude. He wants us to be concerned about people who have needs, especially the poor and hungry, and more than that, He wants us to help in whatever way we can.

°Your family might want to save some money as a family project and send it to one of the several organizations which provide relief for the hungry. For example, contact World Vision International, Box O, Pasadena, California 91109; or Compassion, Inc., 7776 Irving Park Road, Chicago, Illinois 60634; or Food for the Hungry, Box 200, Los Angeles, California 90041.

Questions

a *For Family Discussion:* Why should we be concerned about hungry people when they are mostly overseas and so far away from us? What can we do to help needy people? Try to be practical.

b *For Adult Discussion:* Can birth control really help with the problems of overpopulation and world hunger? What other things could you or your family do about the problems of world hunger? In view of the Bible reading today, can you as a Christian legitimately ignore the needs of other people?

Prayer Suggestions

Thank God for the food that He gives us. Pray for the hungry of the world and ask God to show us how we can help them.

Part 9

Life Before Birth

Dr. C. Everett Koop, a world-famous pediatric surgeon, once made the interesting suggestion that we are a schizophrenic society.

> We will ship food to a starving nation overseas, and, at the same time, supply arms to its enemy. We will feed another starving people beset by famine, but we will make no attempt to ask them to try to control their population by contraception. We will stop a cholera epidemic by vaccine in a country unable to feed itself, so that the people can survive cholera in order to die of starvation.°

In spite of such inconsistencies, people in our society tend to have a high respect for life. We attempt to keep premature babies, sick people, and the elderly alive. We generally respect the commandment which tells us "Thou shalt not kill," and we are concerned about protecting ourselves and each other from accidents, crime, or illnesses which could bring loss of life.

When it comes to unborn babies, however, our respect for life seems to evaporate. To quote Dr. Koop again,

---

°C. Everett Koop, *The Right to Live; The Right to Die* (Wheaton: Tyndale House Publishers, 1976), p. 17.

"While we struggle to save the life of a three-pound baby in a hospital's newborn intensive care unit, obstetricians in the same hospital are destroying similar infants yet unborn" through the practice of abortion.

Abortion is a controversial issue—perhaps the most controversial topic in this book. Much of the controversy concerns the moment when human personhood begins. Does it start at conception, does it begin at birth, or does it commence at some time in between? If it begins at conception, then all abortion is a form of murder—the killing of defenseless newborn humans. If personhood begins later, then abortion is something less than the destruction of a human being.

Equally controversial is the issue of "exceptions": Are there times when an abortion is justified (in pregnancies that result from rape, for example, or where the mother's life is in danger)? These are the issues we will discuss this week. Hopefully we can reach some conclusions about a topic which has implications for all Christians and their families.

We acknowledge that Christians differ in their view concerning the time when personhood begins.

Read: Jeremiah 1:1, 2, 4-10

There are some people in the Bible that we know a lot about. Moses, Jesus, and Paul, for example, are pretty well-known, and even little children have heard about David and Goliath, Daniel in the lions' den, or Jonah, who was swallowed by a big fish. But what do you know about Jeremiah?

In the Old Testament we read about the prophets. These were men whom God chose to preach to the people and to tell what God wanted them to know back in the times when there were no Bibles. Jeremiah was one of these prophets. For over 40 years he preached to the people, but nobody wanted to listen. They laughed at Jeremiah because he said some things they didn't want to hear. Many people ignored him and nobody wanted to be his friend. The only friend Jeremiah had was God, and day after day the prophet obeyed the Lord even though everyone criticized.

In the Bible reading today we read about the time when God called Jeremiah to be a prophet. It wasn't when he was a young boy or even when he was a teenager. God called Jeremiah before he was born. In fact, God called Jeremiah when he was still in his mother's womb—even before he had begun to form into a head, arms, legs, and a little body.

When do you think Jeremiah first became a person—when he was born or at some time before that? That's a hard question to answer, but certainly God knew and called Jeremiah to be a prophet even before his body was formed. God knew us that early too (Psalm 139:13-16).

After Jeremiah was born and had grown old enough to

talk, the Lord came to him one day and said, "Jeremiah, I want you to speak to the world for me."

It isn't surprising how Jeremiah reacted. "I can't do that," he said. "I'm far too young!" But God touched the young man's lips and gave him the words to say.

Many years have passed since that time. Jeremiah has died and so have all the people he knew. But God is still alive. He still knows all about us. He knew us even before we were born, and He gives us exactly what we need in order to obey and serve Him. Maybe that's a good reason to thank God. He never changes and He knows about us—even when people laugh at us, ignore us, or treat us unkindly, like they did with Jeremiah.

Questions

a *For Family Discussion:* Jeremiah obeyed God but he was criticized by other people. Do Christians get criticized today? Why? When did Jeremiah first become a person—when he was first born or before?

b *For Adult Discussion:* When does personhood begin? Is it at the time of conception, at the time of birth, or at some other time? How do these questions have a bearing on the issue of abortion?

Prayer Suggestions

Thank God that He made us. Thank Him that He knew us before we were born and knows us now. Ask Him to help us be obedient, like Jeremiah, even if people dislike us because we are Christians.

Day 2

We agree that God has admonished us to choose life instead of death and has set penalties for those who would, even accidentally, cause a pregnant woman to be injured in such a way that an unborn child is harmed.

Read: Psalm 8

Several years ago, one of the Russian cosmonauts talked to some reporters following his trip into space. "When I was up in the sky traveling through space," he said, "I never saw God. This proves that God doesn't exist."

Now when you stop to think about it, that cosmonaut's statement is pretty foolish. Just because *he* didn't see God is no proof that God does not exist. There are a lot of things in the world that I've never seen (perhaps you haven't seen them either), but these things still exist. I've never seen Moscow, electricity, an Australian koala bear, or Jimmy Carter, but I know these all exist. And God exists too!

Not only does God exist, but according to our Bible reading today, He made everything—including the world, the stars, and the skies through which that cosmonaut flew in his spaceship. After He created everything. God didn't leave us alone. He is still in control of the universe and the earth, but He let men have charge of everything in the world—the animals, the plants, and everything else.

Sometimes we humans haven't done a very good job in looking after the world that God gave us. We have been so careless that we've burned down great forests, dumped tons of garbage into our lakes and rivers, dirtied the air with smoke, and wasted important and useful things like gasoline and electricity. Some people have even wasted their lives by laziness, selfishness, too much TV, or crime.

In spite of this, isn't it good to know that God cares about the world, the animals in it, and the people like you and me? He loves children and is even concerned about babies before they are born. Once God said that we must be careful not to let pregnant women get hurt, lest the unborn baby get hurt so that it dies (Exodus 21:22). Even unborn babies are important to a God who really cares about everything in the universe.

When a baby is born into a family, everyone gets excited. The parents sometimes send notices to all their friends, pictures are taken of the new baby, and people send gifts to the family to help them celebrate the birth of their child. As far as God is concerned, however, that little baby began to grow long before he or she was born. Birth is really the baby's coming out from the mother's womb into the world. Making babies is part of God's work. He even made the cosmonaut who thinks God doesn't exist.

Questions

a *For Family Discussion:* Do you think God is still in control of the world when there are wars, murders, fires, and people who think God does not exist? If God exists why do you think He permits these things to happen? Might it be that we can't really answer that question?

b *For Adult Discussion:* Read Exodus 21:22, 23. Does this seem like an unjust law? What does it say about God's view of unborn children? What does it say about His view of life and death?

Prayer Suggestions

Today let's praise God—like the writer does in Psalm 8. Thank Him that He exists and that He is mighty, powerful, and in control of the earth. Thank Him that He created the world, including people like you, me, and even unborn babies. Thank Him that He pays attention to us and cares for us even though we are such puny little creatures in God's huge universe.

Day 3

We believe that compassion for distressed mothers and families, and concern for unborn children, require us to offer spiritual guidance and material solace consistent with the teachings of God's Word.

Read: Luke 10:30-37

Have you ever heard of Eleanor Bradley? Probably not, because she wasn't very famous except for the day when she fell on a busy street in a big city.

Eleanor Bradley was a neatly dressed lady who had gone shopping one morning, but accidently slipped and broke her ankle. Lying on the sidewalk, dazed and in pain, she called for the people around to help, but nobody stopped. "I thought she was drunk," one man said later. "Nobody else was helping her," said another man, "so I just assumed nothing was wrong."

Eleanor Bradley lay on the sidewalk for more than 40 minutes before a taxi driver stopped, helped her into the taxi, and took her to the hospital.

At some time in Sunday school most people have heard about the Good Samaritan. It was he whom we read about today. He came along (with a donkey instead of a taxi) and helped the wounded man who had been beaten by thieves and left lying on the road. Before this, however, two religious people had walked by the wounded man and hadn't paid any attention to him. "Let him die," they must have thought. "We haven't got time to stop."

I guess things haven't changed much since the time of the Good Samaritan. Eleanor Bradley discovered that! Even people who are religious sometimes get so busy with their work that they don't have time or don't make the effort to help other people.

Think of the families in your church or in your neighborhood, for example. Do some of them have problems—broken homes, sick children, unhappiness? How do you react to these families? Do you ignore them and (even worse) spend a lot of time criticizing them? Or are you like the Good Samaritan (or the good taxi driver) who tried to help?

It is true, of course, that some families don't want help. Some are too embarrassed to admit their problems, and others might get angry if you offered to help them. Even so, we can show our concern (instead of criticism) for the hurting families we know. We can pray for them, and we can ask God to meet some of their needs by working through us. It is important to think of how our own families can get better, but it is also important for us to help families around us. Jesus was kind to others, and He expects us to do the same.

Questions

a *For Family Discussion:* Why do people today not want to help others? Can there be dangers in helping people in need? What are some of these dangers? Can you think of some families with problems? How can you and your family help them?

b *For Adult Discussion:* What are the advantages and disadvantages of a family or individual offering spiritual guidance and material solace consistent with the teachings of God's Word? Are there specific and practical ways in which you can offer such guidance and solace?

Prayer Suggestions

Thank God that He is compassionate. Ask Him to make us concerned about others, including other families. Pray for some family you know that has problems. Ask God to show you how you could help another family.

Day 4

We urge the church to influence the social-moral climate in which unwanted pregnancies occur.

Read: 1 Corinthians 10:1-5, 12, 13

There have been a lot of books and movies lately dealing with the devil. These books and movies sometimes talk about demons, and they often show how Satan can cause all sorts of problems in our lives.

I think there are a lot of people, however, who don't take the devil and his demons very seriously. Even the people who read these books or watch the movies tend to treat the devil as a joke. They think he doesn't really exist.

However, the Bible says that Satan is a real person who goes about causing trouble, especially for Christians. When the children of Israel were led out of Egypt, God had a lot of good things planned for them, but the people were disobedient. They rebelled against God and did things which didn't please Him at all. As a result, many of the people died in the wilderness. I'm sure this pleased the devil, and it is likely that he encouraged them to be disobedient in the first place.

Do you realize that the devil is still active today? According to the Bible, he goes around like a roaring lion trying to find people to hurt and destroy (1 Peter 5:8). "But the devil isn't interested in me," you might think. "He wouldn't cause me to fall into sin."

But he *is* interested in you, and me, and everyone else. He tries to get people to kill, steal, lie, and hurt others. But he also gives us ideas about being unkind, critical, dishonest, and gossipy.

Another place where the devil gets to a lot of people is in the area of sex. He tempts us to think wrong thoughts about our bodies and the bodies of other people. Sometimes he leads people to have intercourse when they are not married, to show all of their bodies to other people, or to think about how other people might look or act if they were nude. Many people especially teenagers and older adults, have a lot of trouble trying not to think thoughts or do things with their bodies which might displease God.

There is some good news in all of this, however. Most people have had the exact same sexual problems that you might have, but God knows about these temptations. He has promised to help us stand up to the devil and say "No!" even when down deep we really would like to sin by thinking and doing things which are wrong.

We are not left alone to fight the devil. If we were alone, we would surely lose, but God sent His Holy Spirit (who is stronger than Satan) to help us fight. When we are surrounded by other Christians and are doing things for God, we also have help in saying no to the devil. We can even fight these temptations around us which cause people to sin. The devil tries to convince us to do things—especially with our bodies—which displease God, but God offers to help us do what is right. We can choose to obey God or Satan. Which do you do most?

Questions

a *For Family Discussion:* How does the devil work in you or your family, causing you to do things which are wrong and harmful? How can we prevent the devil from doing his work? How can we help others say no to Satan?

b *For Adult Discussion:* Reread 1 Corinthians 10:13. What does this say about sexual temptations? Can family members help each other with problems in this area, or do we need to get help from people outside the home? How can the church influence the social-moral climate in which we live?

Prayer Suggestions

Thank God that He understands our problems and urges us to do things which are not sinful. Ask Him to help all of us not to sin 1) with our minds, 2) with our lips, and 3) with our bodies. Pray for our country, so that things which make people sin will be changed.

Day 5

We see no grounds on which Christians who are concerned for all human life and for the well-being of the family can condone the free and easy practice of abortion as it now exists in our society.

Read: Luke 1:39-45, 56-66

How old were your parents when you were born? Whatever their age, they probably were not as old as Elizabeth and Zacharias. When this couple had their first child, the Bible says, Zacharias and his wife "were both very old," so much so that they were surprised when they learned that they were soon to become parents. Very old women usually don't have babies, but God made this possible for Elizabeth.

Three months before the baby was to be born, Elizabeth had a visitor. When the visitor arrived (it was Mary, Jesus' mother), the baby in Elizabeth's womb jumped for joy.

Do you suppose that unborn baby was already a person when he leaped inside his mother's womb? I'm sure Elizabeth thought he was, but did you know that unborn babies like that are killed every day in many hospitals in our country?

In an operation called "abortion," these unborn babies are removed from their mother and either killed by the operation or allowed to die. If any mother in the United States today wants an abortion, she can easily get one. The unborn baby, who can't talk and isn't old enough to know what's going on, dies whether he or she wants to or not.

Can you imagine what would have happened if Elizabeth had decided to have an abortion? Her son, John the Baptist, who leaped for joy in his mother's womb before he was born, would never have been born. If Mary had had an abortion (because she wasn't married yet) Jesus would never have been born. And what would have happened to you if your mother had decided to have an abortion before you were born?

When God gave us the Ten Commandments He told us not to kill, and once a baby is born we try to obey this rule. But what about the baby who isn't born yet? Does abortion mean that we are really killing unborn people? There are many people who think this is so, but others don't think abortion is the same as killing at all. Whatever you think, I'm sure you agree that it isn't pleasing to God when thousands and thousands of abortions take place in the world every year—sometimes just because a man and woman decide that they don't want the bother of another child. I think that is wrong, don't you?

Questions

a *For Family Discussion:* Is abortion *always* wrong? Are there times when abortion might be all right?

b *For Adult Discussion:* Do you think abortion is really a form of murder? Is abortion always to be condemned, or are there certain legitimate causes for abortion? What is your attitude toward the free and easy practice of abortion as it now exists in our society?

Prayer Suggestions

Thank God that He is concerned about life and that He protected us before we were born. Ask Him to give us the right attitude toward abortion—an attitude which pleases Him.

Day 6

We exhort the church to show compassion for those who suffer because of the abortion experience.

Read: Matthew 14:1-21

Yesterday we read about the birth of John the Baptist, and in our Bible reading this time we read about his death. Can you explain what happened? John obeyed God by telling King Herod that the king had sinned. The king didn't want to hear this, so he threw John into jail and later had his head cut off.

This must have made Jesus very sad. He went off by Himself to think and pray after John's death, but before long there was a big crowd looking for Jesus and wanting Him to heal the sick.

Did you notice what Jesus thought about this crowd? He felt sorry for them, and when they were hungry He was concerned about how they would be fed. Jesus was like that—always concerned about people and wanting to help them, even when they were sick, sinful, or not able to understand Him.

This week we have talked about abortion. We have said that it is like killing an unborn baby, and yesterday we decided that abortion is often (many people would say always) wrong. Now suppose some lady has an abortion and decides later that she made a mistake. Suppose some doctor or nurse works on an abortion and decides later that this was wrong. Suppose some husband or other person encourages a woman to have an abortion and afterwards thinks this was a terrible mistake. These people all feel bad about the abortion, but by then it is too late to do anything about it. The unborn baby is gone, and he or she cannot be brought back to life again.

How do you think Jesus would have treated these people who feel so badly about some abortion? Would He have yelled at them or told them they were bad? No! Jesus loved people and showed a concern for them. Even if He had thought the abortion was wrong, He would have forgiven them (if they had wanted to be forgiven) and He would have been concerned about them.

Like John the Baptist, Jesus was killed as an adult, but He rose again and now is alive in heaven. Since He no longer lives on earth in a human body, He wants us to show compassion, concern, and love to people who are sad, angry with themselves, or hurting. We've got to be loving to all people, including those who suffer today because of an abortion that they or somebody else had in the past. It's the Christian thing to do.

Questions

a *For Family Discussion:* Why do you think an abortion might cause adults to suffer or be sad? What can you do to help these unhappy people?

b *For Adult Discussion:* Why does abortion cause suffering? How can the church show compassion for those who suffer because of the abortion experience? How can you or your family show such compassion? Be specific. Why should we be compassionate?

Prayer Suggestions

Thank God that He is loving and concerned about us. Pray that you or your family will be loving and compassionate too.

Part 10

Stained-Glass Windows & Freckly-Faced Kids

I'm not sure where I saw it, but several years ago I came across a painting of two little kids in church. They were freckled, well-scrubbed, neatly dressed, and very pious-looking as they sat in the pew with a stained-glass window in the background.

I don't know anything about the painter, but I suspect that he or she didn't have any kids. Children, I am convinced, rarely sit still and pious in church. They wiggle and have difficulty both maintaining interest and sitting still—especially during long sermons.

Perhaps, however, that painting of worshipping

children expresses an ideal—an ideal of families united together in church, serving and worshipping God. But many families miss this ideal. They find church boring, get little support or encouragement from church members (and give even less support), see no real need for the church, and don't have much rapport with other members and families in the local body of believers.

Some churches even foster disunity. They have men's meetings, women's groups, and a variety of children's activities which divide the family instead of uniting it, especially when these activities occur on different nights of the week.

Instead of this, the church should be pulling families together and joining them with single people to form a unified, healing, caring, mutually supportive group of believers. All of us need this. Going our independent ways, as we are inclined to do in this busy age, is destructive and not what God intended for His people. Think about this as you read the last paragraph of the Affirmation and work through this last part of the book.

Day 1

We affirm that the family as a unit is not self-sufficient and self-contained as a body of believers. Rather, the family has need of continuing support from other families and from individuals within the Body.

Read: Ephesians 3:1, 13-16

Not long ago I got a letter from a man who is in jail. He wanted me to send him some books, but in his letter he also told me about some of his problems. He didn't tell me what crime he had committed, but he did say that being in jail isn't very pleasant.

When the Apostle Paul was in jail, he didn't find it very much fun either, but in a letter written to his friends he said that some things made him happy. He was glad, for example, that preaching about Jesus was the reason he got put in jail, and he was happy to know that God was right there with him to help in his sufferings. Paul, as you know, wasn't married, but he was part of a family—a family of Christians ("some of them already in heaven and some down here on earth"). The family of Christians on earth prayed for Paul, and he also prayed for them, even when they couldn't see each other.

Can you imagine how lonely it would be if you were all alone without a family, or if yours was the only family in the whole world? There was a family like that once—the family of Noah. After the flood was over and the animals had been let out of the ark, Noah, his wife, his three sons, and their wives were the only people in all the earth. They had each other, and that was good, but there wasn't anyone else. They weren't like Paul or like the man in jail who wrote me the letter. Even in prison Paul knew that there were many other people who had the same heavenly Father that he did, and who were part of the great family of God.

At the beginning of this book we talked about the fact that every Christian is part of two families: the family we live with or came from, and the family of God. Our own little families can't get along very well if they are alone. Each of our families needs other families to help us, encourage us, and be with us in times of fun and in times of trouble. Even when we are far away from our own families (like the man in jail is away from his family) or when our family members have all died, we still remain a part of God's family. And we can meet with other members of God's family whenever we go to church.

Someday all the members of God's family will get together in heaven. Jesus will be there and so will God, our heavenly Father. We'll all be dressed in fine clothes, and we'll have a family dinner which is bigger and better than any family dinner that we've had on earth at Christmas or Thanksgiving.

Until then, however, we who are in God's family should worship together, spend time together, and help other families in our church. We should also thank God that there are other families around—unlike in the days of Noah, when all he had was his own wife and children.

Questions

a *For Family Discussion:* Why do families need other families? How can your family help another family? What can another family (or families) do to help you?

b *For Adult Discussion:* According to the Affirmation "the family has need of continuing support from other families and from individuals within the Body." Do you agree? Why? How can families "within the Body" support each other? Be practical and specific in your answer.

Prayer Suggestions

In our Bible reading today did you notice that while he was in jail, Paul prayed for the other Christians in God's family? Today let's thank God that our family is not the only family there is. Then pray for one or two other families in your church. Pray for a missionary family too—away from home but still part of the family of God.

Day 2

The local church is a company of believers who exist for fellowship, worship, teaching, and the development of spiritual gifts to the end that God will be glorified and the Body of Christ edified. As part of the universal Body of Christ, the local church is an extended family composed of nuclear families (and individuals who are living apart from nuclear families).

Read: Acts 2:1-8, 12-18, 40-47

When did the first family begin? It started in the Garden of Eden, when God created Adam and Eve as the first husband and wife. Soon they had children, and within a few years there were many people (and families) on the earth.

In our Bible reading today we read about the time when the first church began. Several days after Jesus had gone up into heaven, the Holy Spirit came into the lives of the Christians, and everyone was amazed.

It is interesting that some of the people there decided that the disciples must have been drunk. I don't know if drinking was a problem at the time of Jesus, but it is a problem today. In the United States alone, about 9 million people are alcoholics, and of these about half a million are teenagers. This is a sad problem which ruins many families. It is a problem which we can avoid if we don't ever start drinking in the first place, and it is a problem for which we can get help from counselors in our community. But this wasn't the disciples' problem.

They were learning for the first time what it is like to have God's Holy Spirit in their lives. Peter, one of the disciples, decided to tell the crowd what was happening, so he began to preach a sermon outside, right in front of the crowd. When he was finished, 3000 people decided to "turn from sin, return to God, and be baptized in the name of Jesus Christ."

Then the disciples *did* have a problem. Suddenly there were 3000 new Christians who wanted to go to church. Since they didn't have church buildings then, the people broke up into smaller groups and met in homes. There they praised God together, shared their meals with each other, helped one another with their needs, and learned to enjoy being together with other believers. At times they also came together in a large group to worship, listen to the disciples' teaching, take part in communion services, and pray.

There must have been many families in this early church. Often they had other families and individuals in their homes, and they must have known that the church of Jesus Christ is made up both of people who are living with their own (nuclear) families, and of those who are living away from their families. All of these people had different abilities and gifts from God, but they had one purpose in life—to bring glory to God and to build up one another in the church.

Do you think these early Christians can show us what our families and churches should be like today? As family members and church members we need to be obedient to Jesus Christ, filled with His Holy Spirit, always trying to avoid sin, concerned about the needy, faithful in our prayer and church attendance, and praising God in our homes— having other Christian families and individuals join with us. Read that last sentence over again slowly. It's pretty important.

Questions

a *For Family Discussion:* How can we, as Christians and family members, do each of the things which are mentioned in the last paragraph above?

b *For Adult Discussion:* Reread the last paragraph above. How can we implement each of these suggestions? Should we consider the early church as a model for the church today?

Prayer Suggestions

Thank God that families and churches can work together to help each other. Pray that your family will be concerned about helping other Christians, especially Christians in your church.

Day 3

The Church exists to support, nurture, and equip individuals and families for growth in discipleship (including evangelism) and effective functioning.

Read: Matthew 28:1-10, 16-20

After His death on the cross Jesus was buried in a tomb, but as we know He was raised from the dead and was seen by His followers on the first Easter Sunday morning. How excited the Christians must have been to know that Jesus was alive again! But the people who killed Jesus weren't too happy when they heard about the resurrection. In fact, they didn't believe it—just like many people today refuse to believe it. But Jesus *did* come back to life, and He is still alive today.

After His resurrection from the dead, Jesus didn't stay on the earth much longer. One day He met with some of His followers on a mountainside, spoke a few words to them, rose up into the air, disappeared into a cloud, and went back to heaven. The last words that Jesus spoke on this mountain are very important because they tell us what He wanted us to remember until He comes again.

"I have all the power in heaven and earth," He said. Then He told us to do two things. First, we should "make disciples." This means telling people about Jesus so that they confess their sin and believe that He is God's only Son. Then, second, we should "teach these new disciples to obey all the commands" that Jesus gave to us.

Now who is supposed to make disciples and teach disciples? The answer is *you* if you are a Christian, and the members of your church and family. The church is made up of people who have a job to do. The people in the church must encourage one another, must help each other to become better Christians, and must be trained by the church leaders to go out into the world telling people about Jesus and helping new Christians to obey Christ's commands.

A lot of churches today seem mixed up. They have all kinds of fun activities and interesting projects, but they have forgotten the instructions of Jesus. There is nothing wrong with having fun or working on projects, but we must never forget the most important job that we have to do as Christians: "make disciples" and teach disciples to be obedient.

After telling us this, Jesus made a comforting comment. "I am with you always," He said, "even to the end of the world." Sometimes when we see the sin all around us, it isn't easy to believe that Jesus cares for us, but He does. He is now in heaven, but He is still able to be with us to help us whenever we need Him. That's pretty nice to know, isn't it?

Questions

a *For Family Discussion:* What, according to Jesus, is the most important job for all Christians (read Matthew 28:19, 20 if you have forgotten)? Are you doing this job? Is your family? Is your church?

b *For Adult Discussion:* Does the Great Commission (Matthew 28:18-20) have any relevance for Christian families today? How does it apply to you and your family? Does your church really take the Great Commission seriously? Do you?

Prayer Suggestions

Thank God for the Great Commission. Ask Him to help your family get concerned about telling others about Christ and helping new Christians grow.

Day 4

We urge . . . that families become involved actively in the local church and that they pray, worship, and serve Christ together.

Read: Acts 3:1-11; 4:32-35

The early Christians saw some wonderful things happen. Consider, for example, this report of the lame man who was healed near the Beautiful Gate of the Temple. A lot of people were amazed at what had happened, but the authorities didn't like it, so they promptly threw Peter and John in jail.

The next day they had a trial, but the judges couldn't find anything wrong with the disciples, so they let them go. The Bible says, however, that the judges "were amazed" when they "realized what being with Jesus" had done for Peter and John (Acts 4:13). Being with Jesus had affected the other Christians as well. They began to share what they had with each other, they told others about the Lord, they prayed and worshipped, and they had good times just being with one another. When they weren't at work or worshipping together in houses, the early believers were in the Temple praising God and learning about Him.

In thinking about this recently, somebody in our house asked a very good question. If "being with Jesus" really makes us different, then why should we go to church? Can't we be with Jesus and learn about Him at home?

The answer surely is yes. We can and should learn about Jesus in our houses, and many of us do just that. So why go to church, especially if it's boring or the services are long?

Well, first, the Bible commands us to worship together with other Christians, including other Christian families (Hebrews 10:25). Second, in church we not only get help from others, but we can be helpers to those who need us. For some people, what we give to other Christians in church (in the way of help, encouragement, teaching and money) may be more important than what we get. Then we need to realize that there is value in praying together, worshipping together, and serving Christ together—like the early Christians did.

I think church is sometimes boring, and maybe you do too. The people there aren't always kind or friendly, and sometimes they don't help each other or show much interest in those who are in need. All of this says that Christian people aren't perfect, but still we have a God who can make us better. The place to start changing any church to make it better is with you and your family. And we can't do that if we skip church services and stay home.

Questions

a   *For Family Discussion:* Why should you go to church? Isn't it enough to "be with Jesus" at home? What can your family do to make a church a better church?

b   *For Adult Discussion:* Look up Acts 4:13 and Hebrews 10:25. What practical message might each of these verses have for you and your family?

Prayer Suggestions

Thank God for giving us the church—including your church. Ask Him to show how your family can improve your church. Pray that your church will become more and more a place where individuals and families can "pray, worship, and serve Christ together."

Day 5

We urge churches to minister to families and individuals in creative ways which build church and family unity, prepare young people for mate selection and marriage. . . .

Read: Colossians 1:15-19

Do you have any interest in picnics—especially family picnics?

When I was young our family used to go on picnics every summer, usually on holidays. One of my favorite places was Niagara Falls (which was only a few miles from where we lived). We would watch the water rushing over the edge of the falls, feel the mist blowing in our face, and usually stay around until evening, when they would turn colored lights on the water while crowds of people watched and walked through the park.

Sometimes we had church picnics at Niagara Falls. I never cared much for the games and races, but it was fun riding on the church bus, eating together, and taking part in something where the families who worshipped together on Sunday could enjoy playing together with each other on Saturday.

Now that I am older there are two things about these church picnics that I remember with good feelings. I remember the greatness of the waterfalls which Christ made. I am amazed whenever I stop to look at God's creations. At Niagara Falls the water keeps rushing over the falls even now as you read this, because God controls everything and holds the whole world together. There may be problems on the earth, but we know that the God who created everything, including us, is completely in charge and someday will take all the problems away.

But there is something else I remember about those picnics. It is the good feeling that came when I saw the church members doing things together: traveling, singing, eating, praying. Everybody felt closer to each other after those picnics, and we learned from one another.

Did you notice in the Bible reading today that Jesus Christ is described as the head of a body? Do you know who makes up the arms and legs of that body? It's you and I and our families. God wants us to do things together as Christians—like going on picnics, enjoying God's creation, worshipping the Lord, helping one another, praying for each other, and teaching one another.

The church, for example, is a good place for all of us to learn about marriage, about ways for getting along at home, about God and how we can know Him, and about the importance of living clean lives which please Christ.

Sometimes church picnics can be pretty dull, and most picnics aren't held at exciting places like Niagara Falls. But we in the church should be doing things together, instead of pulling off into our own little family groups and ignoring everyone else in the church except for an hour or two on Sunday.

Questions

a *For Family Discussion:* Does your church and/or family ever have picnics? What do you like about these? How can your family get to know other families in your church? Is there something that your family and another family could do together? Could you include some single people?

b *For Adult Discussion:* Do you really believe that Jesus Christ is in control of the world, including your life? How can the members of the Body of Christ—the church—minister to each other in ways which build church and family unity? Be specific.

Prayer Suggestions

Thank God that He created both churches and families. Ask Him to help churches to improve families, and families to make churches better.

Day 6

We urge churches to minister to families and individuals in creative ways which . . . educate families in effective family living, assist family members and individuals in their spiritual and personal growth, and give support in times of stress or special need.

Read: 2 Timothy 3:1-5; 4:6-8

This is our last session together—our sixtieth meeting. We've discussed a lot during these past weeks: marriage, the family, children, single people, the aged, sex, homosexuality, birth control, abortion, the church, and several other subjects. Now our study is over.

One of the last things the Apostle Paul ever wrote was a farewell letter to his friend Timothy. Paul gave a warning in this letter which we read today in our Bible reading. In the days before Jesus returns, Paul wrote, times will be difficult. People will be selfish, unkind, troublemakers, not interested in their families, not very interested in church, and inclined to ignore God. Doesn't this sound a lot like our world today? Even in our churches and families people are self-centered and not very interested in anyone except themselves.

But Paul wasn't like this at all. He had lived a life pleasing to God, and now he was on his way home to meet his loving Father in heaven. Paul looked forward to the end of his life, and he left word that we too can look forward to meeting the Lord in heaven.

Someday all of us will meet Jesus. He will ask about our lives on earth, and I suspect that He will be interested in our families—how we treated them, how we got along with them, how we helped each other in times of need. Paul had nothing to be ashamed of. Will you?

Maybe we should end this book where we began—by

asking ourselves if we are really members of God's family—people who are sorry for their sins, people who believe that Jesus is Lord, people who want to follow Christ every day of their lives.

Then let's think about our earthly families, and how our families get along with the people around us—especially people in our church.

Most families have problems, but no problem is hopeless. We who are God's children can, with His help, work on the problems and really learn about getting along with our family.

Questions

a *For Family Discussion:* What kinds of problems does your family have? What are you doing to solve these problems? What has each member of your family learned from this book? How will your family be different from now on as a result of having read this book?

b *For Adult Discussion:* Reread 2 Timothy 3:1-5 slowly. How does each phrase relate to your family? What are your most pressing family problems? What are you doing to solve these? Where will you go from here in building family (and church) unity?

Prayer Suggestions

Thank God for your family. Ask Him to help your family improve.

Study Guide

The following questions are designed for adult or teenage discussion of the issues that will be discussed each week on the family. While some of these study questions are similar to what you will discuss at home, most are different and are designed to get you thinking about what will be discussed during the week.

Discussions are most effective when there are few people involved (8 to 12 is ideal), when everyone is free to participate, when the leader lets people talk (a good leader talks no more than 5 to 10 percent of the time), when no one feels pressured to talk if he or she doesn't wish to, and when the leader keeps the group from getting too far off the topic. It is best if participants can agree to meet regularly and to limit the length of meetings to a specific time (say 60 or 90 minutes). Incidentally, please do not feel bound by the following questions. They are merely suggestive and can be supplemented or replaced by other questions if the group agrees.

PART 1 — The Bible and the Family

1. Begin by having a member of your group read aloud Part 1 of the Affirmation on the Family (page 13).

2. What does it mean to say that God is eternal, triune Creator, Sustainer, Savior, and Lord of the universe? How might each one of these descriptions of God have a bearing on marriage and the family today?

3. The second sentence of the Introduction mentions 1) "His great salvation" and 2) the Christian's fellowship with other believers. Do either of these have any influence on your marriage or family? Be honest. Should these make a difference in your home? How?

4. Do you think families are really deteriorating? Give reasons for your answer. What are the influences which most threaten family stability today? What, if anything, can be done about these influences?

5. Is it really feasible to think that the Bible can be an authority and a foundation on which "to build stronger marriages and better family relationships"? How can families like yours use the Bible to strengthen your family? Be specific and practical.

6. Look at the first two sentences of the statement on the origin and purpose of marriage. Each of these words was carefully chosen: instituted by God, instituted . . . at the beginning of the human race, to involve total commitment, lifelong commitment, commitment to God, commitment to each other, involving a man and woman, honorable, involving privileges and responsibilities, mutual submission, companionship, respect, fidelity, sexual fulfillment, procreation. What, in a practical sense, does each of these terms mean to you? Is the list supported by Scripture? Would you add to or subtract from the list? Why?

7. "Marriage is a joyful joining of lives at many levels." What does this mean to you?

8. The Affirmation implies that "mature love" is "vital to the wholeness of persons." What is mature love according to you and according to the Bible? Can we be whole, complete persons without mature love?

9. In practical ways how can we teach children what

paragraph 2 says about the origin and purpose of marriage? Try to be practical and specific in your answer.

PART 2 — How to Be Married and Like It

1. At the beginning of the discussion today have someone read aloud the paragraph in the Affirmation titled "The Uniqueness of Christian Marriage." Now read Ephesians 5:21-23.

2. Describe the relationship of Christ to His church (see verses 25-27, 29). In what ways is marriage like this?

3. "In Christian marriage the husband and wife strive to become one spiritually, intellectually, emotionally, physically. . . ." How can this be done? Be specific.

4. Do you agree that the husband and wife should "function interdependently as equals . . . share equally . . . [and] dedicate themselves to the well-being of each other"? If they are equals, how does this fit with the husband's role as "head of the wife" and Biblical instructions for the wife to submit? Does Philippians 2:5-11 help with your discussion?

5. What does it mean for a husband to be head of the wife? What does it mean for a wife to submit? Be specific and give examples. Honestly now, how do you feel about this teaching in the Scriptures?

6. In what practical ways can the husband and wife encourage each other to "develop their own gifts and abilities"?

7. Many Christian marriages today have deteriorated into "tired friendships"—and sometimes the husband and wife are just tired (not friends). How can Christian couples keep their marriages alive and growing?

8. Should we teach our children about trial marriage, gay marriage, open marriage, and the other contemporary forms of wedlock? If so, how do we go about doing this?

9. What are the best ways to teach your children about

marriage as God intended it to be? What are the things you want your children to know about marriage? (Is your marriage a good model for your children? If not, how could it be improved?)

10. If you are single, does all of this teaching about marriage have any relevance for you?

Part 3 — Marriages That Crumble

1. Begin today by reading the paragraph in the Affirmation titled "Divorce and Remarriage." Then read Matthew 19:1-9 and 1 Corinthians 7:10-14. These are probably the two clearest statements on divorce in the New Testament.

2. Do you agree that "divorce and remarriage are among the factors contributing to the breakdown in family life"?

3. Do you think that "divorce is contrary to God's intention for marriage"? Why, then, is divorce so common in our society?

4. Look at the Scriptures which were read today. Under what conditions, if any, is divorce permissible 1) for a marriage of two Christians, 2) for a marriage of two non-Christians, 3) for a marriage where one person is a believer and the other is not? Give reasons for your answers.

5. Andre Bustanoby, A Christian marriage counselor, has suggested that the following summarizes the Biblical rules of divorce. Do you agree or disagree? Why?

(a) A Christian husband and wife are not permitted divorce and remarriage because they have in Christ the means of fulfilling the ideal of marriage. Divorce *without* remarriage is permitted in 1 Corinthians 7:10, 11.

(b) A Christian and a nonbeliever may divorce if the nonbeliever initiates the divorce. Divorce being a real dissolution of the marriage, the believer is free to marry.

(c) Two unbelievers are permitted to divorce for any cause, and divorce being a real dissolution of the marriage, they are permitted to remarry.

6. How does your church treat separated or divorced persons? Are these people excluded from fellowship and church leadership? If so, are you saying by your actions that divorce is an unpardonable sin?

7. How can we most clearly and effectively teach our children about divorce and remarriage? What do we want them to know?

8. Reread the last sentence in the Affirmation statement about divorce and remarriage. In your church how can you "clearly and persistently" teach about marriage and provide a "therapeutic community of believers"? Are there other things you can do to prevent or reduce the prevalence of divorce in your community? Try to be specific. What will *you* do?

Part 4 — What to Do with the Kids

1. Do you think any children today are really "abused or neglected"? How can this be prevented?

2. What is "healthy self-esteem"? How can this be taught? Does the Affirmation help you to answer? Can a parent teach a healthy self-esteem if he or she has a bad self-image? What can be done about improving the adult's self-esteem?

3. Read 1 Samuel 3:1-18. Eli was a man of God but he had failed in one important area. Why do you think God was so harsh on Eli? Is Eli's case different from that of the Christian parent today who *tries* to raise children in a godly way but fails? Is Isaiah 1:2 of any relevance to our children?

4. How can children be helped to grow mentally, physically, spiritually, and socially? Be specific.

5. How can parents teach the Word of God at home? What do you do about family devotions in your house? What would you like to do that you are not doing now? How can mature Christians (including parents) "teach spiritual truth and other information by word of mouth and by example"?

6. How can we discipline little children effectively? What about mid-age children and teenagers?

7. How can parents teach children to obey? (Read Ephesians 6:1-4). How can your church help parents to train their children in obedience? Be specific.

PART 5 — Happiness Is a Warm Family

1. I suggest that you begin your discussion this week by reading aloud Part 5 of the Affirmation, the section titled "Family Life."

2. What are some practical ways by which closeness and warmth can be developed in families—including your family?

3. What are spiritual gifts? (Read 1 Corinthians 12:4-11). Do you agree with the statement that "each member of the Christian family (*including children*) has spiritual gifts"? How can these be discovered and developed in the home? How can they be discovered and developed in *your* home?

4. The Affirmation statement urges "mothers and especially fathers to resume their God-ordained roles as leaders in the home." How can this be done? (Be specific.) Why do you think that the writers of the statement inserted "especially" before the word "fathers"? Do you agree that fathers should *especially* resume their leadership role at home?

5. Pornography, drug abuse, unethical advertising, television, films, and printed news media are all described

in the Affirmation as "harmful events." In what ways are each of these harmful, and what can we do about each?

6. Read Deuteronomy 6:1-7. What does this imply about adult example in the home? What can a family do to counteract the influence of "poor adult example" and "lack of discipline" in the home and school?

7. How do we get "mature love, respect, and discipline" into our homes? Be practical.

8. Does your church "give priority attention to the task of equipping parents to provide homes in which the spiritual, psychological, intellectual, and social development of children is of crucial importance"? How could your church do a better job of reaching this goal?

9. Is there anything you can or should be doing to help families other than your own to develop warmth and greater closeness?

PART 6 — One-Person Families

1. You might begin your discussion by reading that part of the Affirmation statement dealing with "The Single Person" and "The Widowed and Elderly."

2. What is your real attitude toward unmarried adults? Do you agree that "singleness and celibacy are for some persons gifts from God, preferable to marriage . . ."? If you believe this, does your attitude toward single persons show this?

3. Assume that a single person became a possibility for becoming the pastor of your church. How would you react to having a single pastor? Is your reaction a real indication of your attitudes to singles?

4. Is the local church really a "family of all God's people"—including the single, divorced, and widowed? Are these people fully accepted in your church and encouraged to utilize their gifts? Should they be?

5. Think about the single and aged members of your family. How do you treat them? How *should* you treat them?

6. What are some of the problems faced 1) by the unmarried, 2) by the formerly married, and 3) by the elderly (married or not)? How can families help to solve these problems? What about the church?

7. How can we teach children to respect old people, especially those elderly members of our families? Is parental example a good guideline (i.e., can we assume that if we show respect, concern, and interest in the elderly our children will learn to do the same)?

8. How can your church "minister to the elderly, neglected, lonely, and needy in a spirit of Christian acceptance and concern"?

PART 7 — One Plus One

1. Begin the discussion this week by reading the part of the Affirmation dealing with human sexuality.

2. What does the Bible say about sex? Read 1 Corinthians 6:17—7:5 and 1 Thessalonians 4:1-8.

3. What are the reasons for a "moral decline in our society"? How can we resist this? Be specific.

4. In what practical and specific ways can parents convey the idea that "sexual intercourse within marriage is desirable, honorable, and consistent with personal holiness"?

5. When and how should children and teenagers learn what they need to know about sex? The Affirmation talks about the role of the church in sex education. Where do the church and school fit into this task, and what is the responsibility of parents?

6. What is your attitude toward sex? Can you discuss it openly at home and/or in your group? Is your attitude one of repulsion, thanksgiving, cynicism, celebration, avoid-

ance, or what? As a Christian, what *should be* your attitude toward sex?

7. How can we control our sexual urges and help others to do the same? Does the last sentence of the Affirmation statement on human sexuality give any clues? What is the relevance of 1 Corinthians 10:13? Try to be practical in your answers.

PART 8 — Zero Population Growth

1. We will begin our discussion with the subject of homosexuality. Please read the paragraphs in the Affirmation dealing with homosexuality, then read the following Scripture verses: Leviticus 18:22; 20:13; Romans 1:27; and 1 Corinthians 6:9.

2. What is homosexuality? Is there a difference between "overt homosexuality" (where a couple stimulates each other sexually) and "covert homosexuality" (where an individual thinks homosexual thoughts and is attracted to people of the same sex, but does not engage in any homosexual acts)?

3. Many people today consider homosexuality to be a private matter which is morally neutral and acceptable between consenting adults. What do you think? Is homosexuality a sin? If so, should we reject homosexuals and refuse to admit them into the church?

4. What and how should we teach our children about homosexuality? Is it better to not mention the subject at home? What about mentioning it in church?

5. In what practical ways can we "minister to those who are homosexually oriented in order to help them to change their lifestyle in a manner which brings glory to God"? Assume that someone in your group has homosexual tendencies. What can you say that would help them?

6. What is our reaction to the ease with which contraceptives can be obtained in our society today? Do you think

this encourages premarital or extramarital sexual intercourse?

7. Does the church (including the youth leadership) have any responsibility for teaching young people about birth control and contraceptives? What should be the role of parents in this part of a young person's sex education?

8. The Affirmation statement on birth control points to the reality of overpopulation and world hunger, and the harmful effects that these can have on families and the world. What can your church and your family do about these problems? Try to be specific and practical.

PART 9 — Life Before Birth

1. Begin by reading (out loud) the Affirmation paragraph on abortion. In what ways would you like to see this changed?

2. Were you a person at the time of conception? If not, when does one become a person? What are the implications of this for your view of abortion? Do the Christians in your group "differ in their view concerning the time when personhood begins"?

3. Look at the Bible references which appear at the end of the Affirmation paragraph on abortion. What, if anything, do each of these tell us about abortion?

4. Are there times when abortion is the moral and loving thing to do or is abortion always wrong?

5. Is adoption of an infant a desirable alternative to abortion? What are some other alternatives?

6. What do you want your children to learn about abortion? How can they be taught what you want them to know?

7. How can your church "influence the social-moral climate in which unintended pregnancies occur"? Be specific.

8. Is it the Christian's duty to oppose (politically and in

other ways) "the free and easy practice of abortion as it now exists in our society"? How could this be done?

9. What is your attitude and that of your church toward people whose view on abortion differs from yours? What *should* be your attitude?

PART 10 — Stained-Glass Windows and Freckly-Faced Kids

1. Do you agree that the family is "not self-sufficient and self-contained" but that it needs the church for support in order to maintain stability and growth? If you agree, do you think a noncaring church can do anything for individual families? Does your church really minister to families? If not, why not?

2. According to the Affirmation, "the local Church is a company of believers who exist for 1) fellowship, 2) worship, 3) teaching, and 4) the development of spiritual gifts to the end that God will be glorified and the Body of Christ edified." How can your church accomplish these four goals? Be specific.

3. How can a church "support, nurture, and equip individuals and families for growth in discipleship (including evangelism) and effective functioning"? Is your church succeeding in this task? What are the first steps you should take to do this task more efficiently?

4. Does your church have programs which divide rather than tie families? How can you change this?

5. In what specific ways can your church do each of the following:
   —build church unity?
   —build family unity?
   —prepare young people for mate selection and marriage?
   —educate families in effective family living?

—assist family members in their personal and spiritual growth?

—give support in times of stress or special need?

6. Now that you have finished this book, what can you and your family do to keep building family unity? Where will you go from here? Write down some specific things to do next.